BIG BLACK & UGLY

...... OR SO I THOUGHT

Sha'Kyra Shante' Richardson

Copyright © 2021 Sha'Kyra Shante' Richardson

All rights reserved.

ISBN: 978-0-578-33938-2

DEDICATION

To my children that were there from the beginning to witness all of my downfalls and my glow up. Things may have not always been perfect in our lives however, you all have made my journey worth it. I can never thank you or apologize to you enough, but what I can do is continue to show you the love, support, and encouragement you deserve. None of this would be possible without your consistent grace and love. My goal is to make sure that you always remember who you are, that you are enough, and that you matter.

To my husband, there is absolutely no way that I can begin to tell you how much you mean to me. You always encourage me to embrace my past, to learn from it, and never hide from it. You have always made me feel worthy of all things good. You are everything that I thought I didn't deserve. You have shown me what it is to be loved and to love. To marry someone that allows you to be your authentic self is a gift in itself. Thank you will never be good enough but thank you!

To mom and pops where do I begin? Thank you. Throughout all of my chaos and uncertainty, the only thing consistent and guaranteed were you two. No matter how mad, disappointed, frustrated, or sad you were with me your love never wavered. You two showed me what unconditional love was. No matter how bad I messed up you were always there to pick up the pieces. I never had to guess my place in your lives and for that I thank you. Pops, no one could ever tell me that you aren't my dad and that we don't have biological ties. You have never treated me any different from your biological children. Even when the world turned its back on me, and there were times when you could have too, you didn't. Thank you for never being afraid to call me on my shit!

To the women that may be reading this, know that we aren't much different and if I can overcome so can you. You have been and always will be enough! Allow people to think what they're going to think and move on because what they think about you ain't your business! Never shrink yourself to fit in someone else's box. Most importantly you deserve love, compassion, understanding, and grace. Never forget who the fuck you are!

TABLE OF CONTENTS

I Was Almost A Crackhead	06
This Is Me	10
Slowly Dying On The Inside	46
The Devil Came To Collect	91
Oh Shit! I'm The Toxic Friend	111
Chasing My Monsters	131
Forget Your Failures, Forgive Yourself	142

I Was Almost A Crackhead!

When you think of a crackhead what comes to mind? That they steal, disappear, re-appear at the most inconvenient times, asks to borrow money, can't keep up with their bills, always got an excuse about why they continue to fail at life, never takes responsibility for anything, they are not dependable EVER, they never care who they hurt, and if irresponsible was a person……it would be them… right? All they ever want to do is chase and conquer that next high by any means necessary. I mean if I had to define an addict based on what I have seen, it would be that exact description.

Every attribute of an addict that I listed described me exactly. I mean I've been evicted, wrote fraudulent checks, been homeless, lost my kids, got title loans, car repossessed, and everything in between. The only thing that was missing was the crack! Looking back, I was co-dependent on everything and everyone. They say hurt people hurt people and I was doing just that. I was hurting everyone including myself. Literally, no one was exempt. My high started with attention and progressed to sex, illegal money, partying, men, and so many other things. I was Big, Black, and Ugly! No one had ever given me that title but when I think back, all three of those words defined who I was and who I would become. I allowed that description of myself to dictate my life and my decisions. I always thought I was a lost cause because of all of the mistakes I made in my short time on this earth. On the exterior I faked it, and the "it" can be a representation of so many things. I faked friendships, orgasms, happiness, positivity, forgiveness, and that's just the shortened list. Who knew you could be high on TOXICITY? Although I wasn't actually doing crack, my behaviors led my family to think I was either on crack or crazy. Heck, based on my behavior it's probably safe to assume they thought I was crazy AND on crack.

Life can unravel fairly quickly if you don't check yourself and that's where I went wrong. I was a kid, so I am not sure how much damage control I could have done, but something would've been better than nothing I suppose. I allowed life to drag me for filth for a good 20 years, and I didn't even bother to fight back. I learned how to grin and bear the emotional hurt I transported around day to day. The emotional scars were hidden so well that even to a trained eye they were nonexistent. I had become a professional at packing and carrying my trauma-filled baggage around and calling it a cute purse. I even got good at distributing my shit into my "friends" bags as well. They thought that they were helping me but in reality, I was just transferring my issues and bad habits to them to carry as their own. No one wants to be miserable alone, so the miserable recruit unknowing "friends" that are easy to sway. Sad huh?! As sad as it may be, this was my life.

It took a long time for those bags to get too heavy but

when they did, I was ready. I had to eventually swallow my pride, admit I was wrong, and ask myself for forgiveness. The process was long, tiresome, and I was ashamed when I saw the aftermath of my recklessness. I began to love on myself the way I wished others did. I began to learn what it meant to be valuable. I invested the time in me that I wished others would have. I began to look within. I was the problem and no one but me could fix me. I am so grateful that it is never too late to want to be better and do better. To anybody that thinks it is too late, know that it is NOT! Your past does not have to define your future. Do the work, put your pride to the side, and hold yourself accountable. You owe it to the little girl inside of you! She's counting on you to give her what you couldn't when you were younger.

This Is Me

Sunday, November 8th, 1981 at 3:13 am, a star was born or so my mom thought! Sha'Kyra Shante Amos is what my mother decided on as a name for me, pretty fancy huh? St. Joseph's Hospital in Joliet, IL is where I was born. I came into the world eyes wide open, weighing 7 pounds 15 ounces and 21 inches long. My mom describes me as having skin like rich dark chocolate and hair like silk. I was a perfect ending to a long pregnancy. Being the daughter of a 17-year-old mother never phased me in anyway. I had everything I thought I ever needed and if my mom ever struggled, I never knew it. She was and is literally everything I needed even when I didn't know what I needed. I was loved past infinity by my mother's small family and my father's large family. Word on the street is that my father's older sisters fought over who's house I would get to spend the night over for the weekend. I was the chocolate baby with good hair and well, everybody loved me. My mother always said I was born when mixed babies were the most desired, but there was just something about me that made everyone want me. My mother didn't let me go to many places without her unless it was to my father's side of the family. I can't recall the timeline of my mother and father discontinuing their relationship, but I know it didn't last long after my arrival.

I started my life being a daddy's girl and, in my eyes, he could do no wrong. He could tell me he was coming to pick me up 100 times and each time I would be waiting with excitement in my heart even though the last 99 times he had flaked on me. On the off chance that he did show, we had an amazing time on our way from my mom's house. The fun didn't last long because we were only together for a brief amount of time. He would either drop me off at his parents' home or one of his siblings' houses so that he could prepare for his night. I can vividly remember him getting dressed to go hang out once I got situated. Looking back, it didn't really matter to me because I had a slew of cousins that I could depend on to keep me occupied. My father was 20 when he had me, so the responsibility was not at the top of his list when it came to being a father. Around the age of 4, my father picked up and moved to Atlanta GA, leaving my mother to care for me alone.

After my father left, my life was honestly the same and I didn't notice the hole left in my heart until he would come to visit and then had to leave. When he would come and visit it was like the whole world would stop for me. I can remember the excitement I would feel to see my father walk through any door for a surprise visit. The feeling would not last long though because I knew soon, he would be singing "the goodbye song" at church, and boom just like that he'd be gone. My father came from a very close-knit religious family. He wasn't the only sibling that lived out of state, so anytime they came to visit they would sing in church on Sunday before they left, and they would always sing the same song. "Available to You" by Rev. Milton Brunson and The Thompson Community Singers was the song they sang and what I considered the "the goodbye song". Although I hated the song because of what it represented to me, boy they could harmonize and make it sound so good. There were so many of them that they didn't need any other people to create a choir, they were the choir. Sitting in the pews with my cousins was typically a fun day but not on days like those. I remember sitting in agony holding back tears because I didn't want the song to end because I could vividly remember what happened each time it did. How does a 6-year-old explain she has a broken heart? How does she explain that there's a hole in her heart in the shape of her dad? No one would be able to receive such an extreme statement from a child. Instead of using my words my tears usually did the talking for me. My heart would race as I got one last hug and a goodbye before the weekend along with the sadness became a blur. I knew that I wouldn't see him for a long while and that did something to me that even as an adult I can't really explain. The best way I can put it is that it broke me. Each time he came and went I feel like I lost a piece of myself.

Time went on and being away from my dad became easier each year, I mean at least I pretended like it was easier. I began to get older and my desire to have my father in my life grew, yet somehow his desire to be a part of mine seemed to decrease. Around the age of 8, I started to fly to Atlanta on summer vacations but never felt at home. He eventually married twice making the second time last. For me, life was at a standstill from the first time he left for a new state and for him life was moving forward and getting better. I had convinced myself I had given up on the idea of having a thriving relationship with him but somehow, I still hung onto every tale he told me. I learned early on how to pretend like I was ok and unbothered before being unbothered was a popular saying on social media. I was a straight A student and yet somehow, I can't remember any ceremony, assembly, or school meeting my dad attending, and trust me there were plenty. My mom filled in the gaps where she could, she would always encourage me to keep open communication, but I had honestly lost hope by the time I was in 2nd grade. I firmly believe that my father being part-time was the start of my insecurities and self-esteem issues, I mean if your father can't love you then how can you be worthy of anyone else's friendship, let alone love.

If you recall, I told you how chocolate I was and how everyone fawned over me as a baby. Well apparently, that only works for babies, and I never got the memo. The chocolate skin is only a positive when you are a newborn at least that is what society led me to believe. I never thought negative about my skin tone, I didn't even know I was being judged on it......until I was being judged on it. I didn't know that people judged how cute or ugly you were based on your skin color or skin tone. Then 3rd grade came around and my whole life was changed. I remember it like yesterday, I had gotten my hair done the night before and like any girl with a new hairdo, I couldn't wait to get to school. I had finally built up the courage to tell my friend I had a crush on a boy in our class. I needed to tell her so that she could ask him if he liked me too. I remember him saying so loud "Ewww, I don't like her. She's black like tar!". That day was etched into my brain and stayed that way well into my adult years. I was mortified, to say the least. I remember going home devastated and telling my mom and she reminded me of how beautiful I was, but I couldn't trust her. My mom was light-skinned and in my young mind, there was no way she could understand or relate. That one little jerk had changed the way I thought about myself for years to come. Not only was I too black, but I was also much taller than all the boys in my class. I was 5'9 to be exact and was wearing women size clothes and a size 9 shoe in the 3rd grade. I have been called everything from African booty scratcher, blacky, and midnight to name a few. I had officially confirmed for myself that I was Big, Black, and Ugly and this mindset began to shape me into the person I eventually became and stayed for a long while even into my adulthood.

After my dramatic diss by my crush in my 3rd grade class, my life went from not even knowing what low self-esteem was to having no self-esteem, although I didn't know there was a word for it until later on in life. Not only would I find out what the word meant, but I would soon find out just how much those two little words effected my decisions in my day-to-day behaviors well into my adult years. I hated being dark skin so much that I started researching how to fix me. I had embarked on a journey to find out how to lighten my skin. I mean, I couldn't make myself shorter or smaller, but I for sure could find a way to be lighter…. right? I hated my skin so much that I approached my friend on the playground and told her I had a recipe for making our skin lighter. I had completely forgotten about this until she reminded me in a conversation that we had later in our adult life. She told me that I had told her that if we just put eggs and bleach along with a couple more ingredients then our skin would be lighter if we applied the mixture to our faces. Imagine being so tired of being called blackie, midnight, tar baby, or darkie that you decided you would make a concoction to lighten your skin. I was a kid for God's sake not a scientist, but I didn't care because I was desperate. I never went through with the skin lightening, maybe I just got distracted with the multiple other things I began to find wrong with myself, so I lost focus. Good thing my friend had enough good sense to decide against trying it as well. Most kids at this age worry about forgetting their lunch or being embarrassed for getting the wrong answer, but for me, I felt like I had the weight of the world on my shoulders.

To add to my troubles, in 3rd grade I started to get these tremors in my hand. I couldn't hold them steady even if I focused very hard. I couldn't pick up drinks without them spilling, I couldn't write legibly, and that's just the shortlist of things I couldn't do. This new issue just came out of nowhere. My mom took me to the pediatrician, a neurologist, and anyone else who would listen. My mom took me to be examined and diagnosed many times to no avail. No one had any idea what was causing my tremors. My mom even went so far as to make me sit and practice holding my hands still and that didn't work either. I was mortified to even be around people even my own family because everyone wanted to know what was wrong with me. The good thing is it came and went, and I was able to hide it most times. I mean I didn't want to be the ugly girl with shaky hands because being the ugly girl was too much by itself. I got really good at hiding my tremors, but it created an anxiety in me that even I couldn't explain. Being around people made me uptight, self-conscious, and anxious. I didn't want anyone to see I had shaky hands because then I'd have to answer a million questions that I didn't even have answers for. I hid it well but exchanged shaky hands for sweaty hands, sweaty armpits, and just overall awkwardness. The tremors started right as 3rd grade was ending so I had somewhat caught a break.

Summertime was always a time that I loved, and the pressures of school didn't matter at least at that moment. We played from sun-up to sundown just being kids. I had a group of friends so being judged was never an issue during the summertime for the most part. No one cared that I was ugly or that my hands shook as long as I could play tag, jump rope, and swing at the playground. I lived very close to my school that doubled as the hang out spot for the summer. We would meet up at the park, walk to the store, talk, play school, and everything in between. It was a carefree summer, and no boys were allowed. I was finally able to be a carefree kid again. I didn't have a care in the world and well 4th grade would be better because summer was simply amazing. I was cured from what I now know as low self-esteem. Nothing that a good summer with my girlfriends couldn't fix right....

WRONG! Life just continued to throw curve ball after curve ball at me and I was never able to recover.

I remember hanging with my friend at her house in the basement. Literally the only friend's house I could visit. We would laugh and talk and just be kids. She had to run upstairs to help her parents one day and I stayed downstairs. Her older brother came and felt on my butt. I recall thinking hmmmm I don't know if this is ok but, I giggled out of nervousness and sat down. He came and sat next to me and then he started telling me I was so pretty. I wanted to hear those words out of someone other than my mother's mouth so bad it was almost as I knew it was wrong but accepted for that reason alone. My friend came back down, and things proceeded as it never happened. I went home that day smiling. This behavior went on each time I went over if he had the chance. I actually looked forward to our interactions because who doesn't love a good compliment. One day those compliments and butt touching went so far left that even my attention starved self was stunned. I can't really recall where my friend was, but the brother and I were sitting on the couch in the basement alone.

He told me that I should put my hands on his hands, and I did. UGH, I should've known better. He put his other hand in my pants and began to massage places I didn't even know existed. My heart was beating, and I felt like I couldn't swallow. The words I wanted to formulate just wouldn't come out. I did not like this, and I knew it was wrong. I try and take his hand out of my pants, but he was way too strong, he was hurting me. He unbuttoned his pants and put my hands in his pants massaging himself with my hand until he ejaculated. At the time I didn't know what that meant but looking back that's exactly what happened. It all happened so fast. He was maybe 18 or 19 at the time and I was 10 maybe. I had never even thought about sex or had any interest in sexual activity EVER! I felt so disgusted and as I snatched my hand away, he said, "You ok chocolate?". My head was spinning, and I had semen all over my hand. I jumped up and wiped my hand on the couch and kind of stood there. My house was around the corner from my friends, so I ran out the basement door and made a beeline for my front porch. I couldn't breathe and I'm not sure if it was because I ran home or because I was having a panic attack. I replayed the scenario repeatedly and figured that if I told my mom she would flip out on me or him and I'd be embarrassed so I kept it in. I went over a few more times and anytime he had a chance he would fondle me or make me fondle him, until I just stopped going over completely. Weird thing is he never told me not to tell but somehow, I never opened my mouth. I was confused as to what this would mean for my friendship with his sister, so I remained silent, but I never returned to their house to play. I was forever changed even though I tried not to even think about it, I did all the time. I kept going back over so I must've insinuated that I liked it. I never said no so that clearly was me saying yes, right. I couldn't help but think that I was overreacting with the feelings I was having. I never told anyone so now it's definitely too late to say something because they'll just think I was lying. I just could not for the life of me process it and I tried, I really tried. How could I have been so stupid, was what my little brain told me. I knew what would fix this and give me resolve, I'd just pretend like it never happened, and I did just that. I never told a soul.

Summer break had come and gone, and 4th grade was

smacking me in my face before I knew it. I walked into the first day of school with sweaty palms, I was a nervous wreck. Everything in my head told me to turn back around and go home, but I knew that what greeted me once I arrived would be no easier than what awaited me in the classroom. Not only was I the same shade of extra crispy black but I got taller, much taller! How is it that I got taller, and the boys stayed the same height? I mean, I was a walking target so you couldn't miss me. I was 5'11, I wore a size 10 in women's clothing, I weighed 160 pounds, and wore a size 10 in women's shoes. Apparently, I was taking the lead in the Big, Black, and Ugly club very seriously. My body was working against me. I asked myself daily how did this happen to me... why me? I mean for God's sake, my mom was a small woman barely 5 foot 6, 115 pounds soaking wet. My dad wasn't big either, he was 5'9 maybe 180 pounds, give or take, when I was growing up. So how did I become so big, I had to be adopted because this just did not add up. I was literally the tallest person in my class, and I hated every minute of it. I went from loving everything about school to never wanting to be there, wishing I could just find a way to convince my mom to let me quit. That school year I just wanted to be invisible, and I tried my damnedest to make sure that happened. I was the queen of around the world in math and had an answer to all the questions my teacher answered, but this year I had no interest. I was always the smartest in class so getting straight A's was an easy task and that didn't change but my willingness to raise my hand did. That school year went off without any disasters, but I was still happy to know that it had come to an end.

Before I knew it, I was in 5th grade and time had flown by. Our fifth-grade dance was coming up and ever since the first grade I had been looking forward to attending this dance. This dance was to signify that elementary school was coming to an end and junior high school was in the very near future. Graduating fifth grade always made me feel like I was no longer a kid but somehow a young adult. All the younger kids looked up to us and couldn't wait to be in our spot. I guess it goes without saying that the fifth-grade dance was a very important milestone. My mom was the best, she was just as excited as I was, little did she know I was also terrified. You see, I never fully told her the struggle that I was having.

I never thought that she would understand because she was so light skin and pretty. Moms have this weird way of thinking that if they tell you you're beautiful, anything else that anyone else said wouldn't matter. Boy was she wrong! In my head, she was obligated to tell me that I was pretty because what mom tells their kid that they're ugly? None! We shopped over the weekend for my dress and accessories. My mom was able to find the cutest little black dress before little black dresses were thing. The dress was a black cotton above knee-length dress with a silver zipper that went from the top down to the breast area of the dress. Don't worry the zipped was for looks only, it didn't really unzip. It was a little formfitting, but nothing too grown up. You know, growing up in a black household anything too grown was frowned upon. I mean my mom went all out for this fifth-grade dance. I think she knew how important this was to me, so it was important to her, my mom was cool like that! The night before the dance I got my hair done by our hairdresser, it was beautiful. I had always had hair down the middle of my back so when people did compliment me, it was always on my hair. They would always look so perplexed trying to understand how someone clearly not mixed could have such beautiful long 3B hair. You know, the type they considered white people hair. It was long, jet black, and had loose curls. I got home my mom wrapped my hair up, I got my shower, I laid my outfit out on the bunkbed beneath me and laid in bed thinking about how awesome the dance will be until I fell asleep. I woke up and couldn't wait to be the star of the show. I just knew they'd finally realize they were wrong about me being big and ugly. I always struggled with waking up without assistance, but that day was different. I jumped up, brush my teeth, and started getting dressed. I put my tights on first and I followed that up with my black dress. When I finally got all dressed up, the black dress was everything that I thought it would be. The dress hugged me perfectly, and I thought to myself maybe being big like me wasn't such a bad thing. The way that I appeared to myself in my head was totally different from what I was seeing in the mirror. My self-esteem was still at zero but seeing myself in that dress gave me the little bit of confidence I needed to walk into that dance. I got to the dance and people were complimenting everyone. My girls were hype and we complimented one another as well. They loved my outfit, but no one said I was pretty.... well, no one I wanted to hear it from anyway. On the flipside, no one said I was ugly, so I guess it was a win for me and my bruised ego. I had an amazing time dancing and running and playing. Towards the end of the dance my crush walked up to me and said "Damn, yo butt big girl. Let me feel it." I responded and said That's nasty, boy" but in my head I was certainly thinking, wow I have his attention with this outfit on. The creepy brother touched my butt over the summer and my crush complimented my butt, I instantly knew how I could get the attention from the opposite sex. I was quickly learning how to be noticed, even if it was in a negative way. If I couldn't be the cute girl, I'd definitely be ok with being the girl with the big butt and long hair. They had officially created a little girl that had now made the conscious decision to over-sexualize herself. Little did I know this would ultimately destroy me internally and be my downfall.

At 11 years old I became obsessed with my body. I was taller than most, but I had a butt and a little waist. When most kids were throwing on anything to go play outside, I was picking the tightest biker shorts I could find. I thrived on those sexual compliments and attention from the opposite sex. I went from needing to be invisible to needing to be seen in a matter of months. It consumed me and my thoughts. My mom always got cute little biker shorts and larger shirts to go over my butt but when I got outside, I would just tuck the shirt in. I was able to get the attention of grown men and for me, that was a win. I was a kid standing by the basketball court just waiting for a chance at an older boy giving me some sort of attention and it happened every time. At that age, no one ever crossed the line sexually and I was ok with that because the compliments were enough. I always remembered that whatever happened in my friend's basement didn't feel good, so compliments suited me just fine. I no longer wanted to play at the park, I wanted to stand near the basketball court and get as much attention as I could. I had no desire to do anything sexually because the attention was enough for me, at least for the moment. To be completely honest I still really didn't even know what sex was.

I made it through the school year and graduated from 5th grade with honor roll, but little did my mom know shit was going left fast! Eventually, we moved to Naperville, IL and I had to start over. I had to make new friends and remember that I would have to be the ugly friend all over again. To make matters even worse was I didn't even have my girlfriends to be my safe space. My world was turned upside down and I didn't even know how to express how I was feeling. I felt like I was in a never-ending nightmare! I knew that if I was going to survive this move, I had to make friends immediately. There were a lot of kids in my new complex, and we all seemed to be getting along just fine once I got past the idea of having to make new friends. I guess I was right around the age where girls started to become boy crazy. We had crushes and we made it known but for me it was never reciprocated. The scary thought behind this is the fact that I would have been willing to do almost anything to be desired. Thinking back, this obsession started with my 3rd grade crush saying I was ugly. It was like a switch was flipped in my brain and I went into overdrive trying to prove I was pretty by any means necessary. If I could go back in time and tell my younger self just how dangerous this behavior was the story may have ended here.

Naperville, IL was a very white city when we moved there, and the few black kids stuck together for the most part. My insecurities magnified once we got settled and I began to go to school with a predominantly white group of children. Going to school in Joliet I wanted to be smaller and lighter. Going to school in Naperville, made me feel too big, too black, too poor, too ugly, and the wrong race. The blonde hair, blue-eyed girls at my school didn't have to work to get attention. Everyone desired them with no effort on their part. I was still a kid that liked to go outside and play, but I also wanted to see who I could get to pay me some attention. The apartments where we lived had a lot of older teen boys in our complex. They always had friends come visit and I was always somewhere in the mix trying to be seen. They saw me too which was even worse. By the time I really had gotten used to life in the suburbs I was in the 7th grade. I was boy crazy and always in trouble. 8th grade we had new neighbors moving in and with the new family came boy cousins that frequented the new neighbors' house. There was a boy that came over with the cousins that showed me attention like you wouldn't believe. Well, I say boy, but he was about to turn 20 and I was only 12 going on 13. I had his attention and he had mine. I quickly decided that I needed to have sex with him and so I did. I was 13 and he was 21 and he was dead-ass wrong because he knew. I had no clue what I was doing, but I was there in the flesh ready and willing. I couldn't wait for it to be over because I needed to hurry and tell my friends. I had officially reached the pinnacle, I had sex. He got up and threw a couple of dollars to me and I never heard from him again. I was confused because I assumed because we had sex, he was now my boyfriend. Looking back, I had this whole thing so fucked up! I was behaving like I thought an adult should, but in actuality, I was a whole immature child allowing my insecurities to put me in bad situations. If only I had just talked to my mother about my issues instead of feeling like I could handle them myself, a lot of this wouldn't even be an issue. One issue just created another horrible situation for me. I started breaking all the rules. I was always on punishment and never able to see my friends. I was triggered and creating chaos in my family and didn't know how to make it stop. I was forced to go live with my biological father and his new wife and his new family. My mom loved me, but she didn't want to lose me to my bad decisions. Hell, she didn't even know why I was making the bad decisions. I was failing my freshman year and school hadn't been in session for more than two months. She decided that although my dad was absent, he could possibly help me since he had more money and well…maybe I missed my dad. My mom thought maybe I just needed my dad, and I did but I needed him in 3rd grade not 9th grade! She told me that she was willing to be heartbroken for the next 3 years if that meant I got myself together. That in itself was a disaster, but it worked…. kind of!

1996 I had moved to Douglasville, GA in the middle of my freshman year. I moved into a 4-bedroom home with my stepmother, biological father, and sister. I was miserable and felt out of place. When I would come to visit my father for the summer's, my cousins and I had rules, but nothing like when I came back my freshman year. He was now so deep in church; he didn't even remember what life was before he got saved. I couldn't have any secular music playing, I had to fast, and I was forced to read the bible, and write about it. We had both services on Sundays, we had Wednesday bible study, and Saturdays we had what was called cell meetings (bible study jr.). I had gone from no church unless it was when I went to my grandparents to eating, sleeping, and breathing church. I was literally at church from 8 am to 8 pm every Sunday. The adjustments I had to make were extreme and all I could think about was my mom saying once I graduated, I could come back and that was my focus....at least at first.

Moving to GA was the worst day of my life but somehow, I ended up loving it. I loved it not because my father, but because of all the friends I had made. You are probably wondering why living at my dad's was so miserable for me. You're probable thinking, "This is what you wanted right?" You finally got your dad and that is all you talked about initially." Ok boo! I hear you I do so I am going to break it down a little more because whew baby. When the day came for me to leave Naperville, IL it was all a blur. Funny thing is I cannot for the life of me remember if I flew to GA or drove to GA but either way I was crushed on the inside. I was angry because how could my mother abandon me. I was empty on the inside because I felt like the two people who were supposed to love me unconditionally didn't. Each adult in my life had moved on and no longer had any room for me. My mom had married an amazing man and had a baby with him. My stepfather IS my dad, so I had no real complaints about him. My mother never excluded me, she never made me feel unwelcomed, EVER. But hear me out, when a kid is already dealing with self-esteem issues, it's easy to jump into that feeling of abandonment. I felt not wanted, I felt like I was an orphan. It was hard for me to see at the time that my mother literally tried everything to "fix" me. We had tried counseling, tough love, mom dates, sweet love, ass whooping's, and everything in between. She was literally drowning, she needed help so that she wouldn't lose me. Moving in with my dad was that exact feeling of abandonment but for different reasons. As I said before that whole trip was a blur, but I do know that when I got to his home I felt alone, isolated, and miserable. I felt like I had been adopted by strangers who were in it for a check. I was placed in the spare room and absolutely no effort had gone into the room to make me feel welcomed. I mean there was a bed, dresser, and closet.... no decorations or anything. I did not feel like I was a daughter moving into her father's home,

I felt like I was a burden. To be completely honest, I didn't even know what I was getting help with. My bio-dad instantly started in firm and advised me of the rules of engagement especially with the whole church thing. Of course, I had chores which was normal, but there were a few things that didn't feel right. My dad and his wife had a lot of gatherings for church or just social gatherings. They would order food and cook food and the kitchen would be a mess. It's their party that I am not participating in, and yep you guessed it, I was on cleaning duty. I was the help for their gatherings, and I despised it. Cinderella ain't have shit on me! I despised watching their friends' kids for their church meetings and so many other things. Sometimes I got paid for it, but I still didn't have a choice. When you walked around THEIR home, there were photos of everyone except me. I took A LOT of pictures with my mom and at school, which she sent pictures each time, so the fact that I had not one was ridiculous. I was invisible! My sister's room was set up so beautifully, grant it she was a baby but still, I expected the same energy for mine. I was going to be living there as the child of the homeowner, why wasn't I set up the same way? Just from my initial scan of things, I hated it and I hated him for leaving me behind and moving forward as if I was a horrible mistake he wanted to forget. I began to feel more like a burden instead of his 1st born daughter. I wanted him to be excited to see me and I just didn't feel that. So, in that moment I decided I would make him feel exactly like he made me feel. See, at a young age I learned how to become calculated. I decided I didn't care about trouble or him being mad because he didn't care about abandoning me and getting a new family. So, I began to pick up the same behavior and attitude. What can I say, I was a kid that felt lost and abandoned, so I hurt them before they hurt me. They went on to have my brother soon after I arrived, so everything was happening, and I was losing control. I wanted to go back home, I wanted to express to my mom that I was no longer broken, and I was better. I couldn't be better though because I honestly had no idea what the hell was wrong with me. I just knew I kept fucking up everything I touched. My emotions and thoughts were all over the place. I knew that in theory I should have been a complete puzzle but instead my pieces were all over the place. Some pieces I hid, others I lost along the way, and some of them were stolen. I had no idea what being complete looked like.

My relationship with my father was still trash and everything he did rubbed me the wrong way. I felt like I had ruined his fairytale life. I felt like my siblings were living the life I deserved, and I just couldn't get past it. I believe wholeheartedly that my father tried, but he was so wrapped up in church that a disobedient child was a hinderance to him. I was biding my time and so was he. I was counting down the days to graduation and so was he. At 14 I knew I had fucked up so bad, so I knew I was there because of my bad decisions. I also knew that I had some deep-rooted issues that needed to be sorted out, but at the time I felt like my mother was done trying and my father never even started. Again, let me be clear, my mom never abandoned me but in my teenage mind she did. I say my dad never started because he was never a father figure to me. He stepped up when I was in trouble but never just spent time loving me or trying to guide me. Before I moved to Atlanta, we spoke on holidays and birthdays when he would remember to call. Even as a young kid I knew what empty promises were. Part of the problem was me having a fairytale life painted in my head. I was my father's first born and maybe I watched too many Disney shows, but I was supposed to be his little princess. I wanted to be his priority, but his priority had shifted from me to his new family and church. I had no place in his world and I knew that. He had changed and I was a reminder of who he was prior to his new life. I was fighting to remind him why I mattered, and I felt like he was pushing me in the closet to hide me from his new life and friends.

I lived in a mental and physical prison. I couldn't even celebrate Halloween so talking on the phone or dating a boy was out of the question, so I did what I knew how to do…sneak. I couldn't go hang out with friends unless it was at church. I honestly couldn't do anything that normal teenagers did. By the time I moved to GA I had been having sex, so it was only natural that I continue down the path. I never had the dating talk, let alone the sex talk so for me dating was pretty much asking a guy if he wanted to have sex. In every sense of the word, I was damaged. I concluded that if I led with sex, most guys wouldn't care what I looked like, they'd say yes. I got the attention and sexual gratification I desired, and they got what they wanted. Sick as it may seem, I wasn't even having orgasms, I was just going through the motions, but for what? I wasn't having orgasms, but the more sex I had the more addicted I became with sex. I wish someone would have just had a candid conversation with me and so many of my issues could have been avoided. The issue was that no one was a mind reader and I never spoke up about my struggles. I was recklessly going through the motions on autopilot guided by horrible lessons I had taught myself in the short time I have been on this earth. My heart hurts as I type this because had somebody raised their damn 3rd grader right, I'd still be an innocent kid but it's too late for the could've, would've, should've.

9th grade school year had already started so I was a new kid. Although I had a fresh start, I still felt ugly and undesirable to anybody that noticed me. The start of this new school was rocky, and I was very timid and just trying to find my way without being noticed. Eventually, I met and made some amazing friends despite my desire to go back home to Illinois. I had somehow found my smile again, I started to remember what my laugh sounded like. I was having fun, but only at school because when I arrived home, the warden was there to remind me of all the fun stuff I couldn't do. My urge to be so sexual was curbed and I just wanted to be a teenager again but, of course that was short-lived.

My freshman year I made it through without effort, but sophomore year I began to rebel. I became the same person my mom was trying to prevent me from being by sending me there. I got a job that I frequently called off to go hang out. I skipped school, stole money from teachers/students, and well just started being the usual me. I had ONE job and that was to graduate, and I just couldn't do that right, but I didn't care. If me being able to hang out and be away from the prison that I was living in, I was willing to take that risk. See with me, I was so good at pretending I was healed from my insecurities, that before I knew it, they were seeping out of me. Sophomore year I had figured out the attendance system. I knew that as long as I attended 2nd period when they took attendance, I would be ok to ditch the rest of the school day. They took attendance 2nd period and carried it to the office. If you weren't there, then they called home and left a voicemail on your phone. The other classes you would get marked absent for, but only for record of report cards and things like that. I would catch the bus to school and then after 2nd period, I would dip out for the rest of the day. I was so smart that I could do the work and get a decent grade without even trying. The decent grades just kept the teachers from calling home to say, "If she came to class maybe she would pass.". I met this guy at school, and he had my attention. He was always dancing and cracking jokes. I liked him a lot and one of the main reasons was because he was blacker than me. I mean super-duper black. I was intrigued because every girl that I knew liked him. How could that be? He was blacker than me and he was so confident. No one considered him ugly, and I needed to know why. I mean I heard the other kids comment on how dark he was but that didn't stop anyone from wanting to be with him or be his friend. One day I was walking the halls because I didn't have anywhere to skip that day. I saw him coming down the hall and he told me he was about to leave and asked did I want to come with him. Well of course I did, duh. We went to get food and then we went back to his place. We watched a movie and then me being me I asked did he want to have sex. His answer surprised me. He said, "You're not supposed to ask me that." I was so embarrassed. I didn't even know what to say. He said boys are supposed to take the lead and that he just wanted to hang out. I was speechless. I had never been turned down before. I spent the whole day there and we had so much fun. We had to be back on campus, so we left his house, he dropped me off on the side of the building and he went to the parking lot. The next time we skipped he showed me a condom and asked if I still was interested. Funny thing is I wasn't, because no guy had ever been nice to me without sex, so I didn't want it to stop. Instead of saying no I agreed so he wouldn't stop talking to me. Using sex to get what I wanted was my way to feel desired. Being big, black, and ugly over-sexualized me in the worst way. I didn't even like having sex! I told yall I was damaged and broken. We ended up having sex but somehow that never changed our friendly dynamic from his end. The thing that did change was my eagerness to hang out with him. It was almost like once I conquered someone my interest slowly faded. I finally had someone that seemed to like me but after I got what I wanted I no longer liked him. My life was chaotic and confusing!

Junior year came and I just didn't care enough to put the effort in, so I started failing my classes. My dad yelled and he had his wife talk to me and I just didn't care. I felt like she overcompensated and was trying to take the place of my mom and I wasn't having it. One day my counselor called me into his office to let me know that I would not be graduating if I did not make up work and retake two classes by the time junior year was out. My "I don't give a fuck party" came to a screeching halt. I knew that if I did not graduate, I would be stuck in this hell hole an extra year and that was not an option. I NEEDED to get back to my mother, the one that loved me for real. As mad as I was at her, I needed her like I needed air. I got my shit together and I got my shit together immediately. You're probably thinking "She stopped skipping school huh?" Nah, I wasn't that bright, I guess. My father tightened the reigns and in good Sha'Kyra fashion, I found a work around. I began working at Six Flags. On days that I was off I would tell him I had work. I would hang at the park with coworker friends, or I would leave the park to hang out with my school friends. If there was a will there was a way and I always found a way! I made it through junior year alive and back on track, senior year was a breeze too.

June 2, 2000, I GRADUATED! I walked the stage and got my diploma. Like she promised, both my mother and my bonus pops were there the day before graduation to pick me up. They drove 12 hours in their 1996 Honda Accord to see me. When she pulled up to my father's driveway and parked, I couldn't contain my emotion. I peeped out the window and sobbed. She didn't abandon me, and she kept her word. I felt the love coming from her car before I made it down the stairs. That hug took away all the pain in my heart for that moment. I couldn't stop staring at her. My bonus pop was there to celebrate me as well. He looked like he was so proud of me. My dad had cake and his church friends over to help celebrate, we stayed maybe an hour and I went back to the hotel with what I can best describe as my real parents. I had plans to go to party with my friends, but of course, my father said I was not allowed. So instead, I packed my shit and stayed at my parents' room. I graduated the evening of June 2, 2000. I was on my way to Chicago before the sun came up on June 3, just like my mom promised. After I left GA, I can't remember the next time I spoke with my father. I was no longer that 14-year-old that left my mom's house, I was now an 18-year-old young adult. I had made it through what I thought was the worst time of my life. I had no idea life would get even more difficult in the years to come. Some by the hands of others and a lot because of me. What!? You didn't think I got my shit together and lived happily ever after, did you?

Slowly Dying on the Inside

The journey back home was filled with tiredness, anticipation, and sadness because I really missed my friends from Atlanta. You would be surprised how kids ain't loyal lol. My old friends from Illinois had moved, went off to college, or had kids which meant no time for me. How do I keep finding myself starting over? I had learned to adapt in any situation, so I had new friends in no time. You ever have all these big plans and when it finally comes to light, its nothing like what you expected? Yea that was exactly how moving back home to Illinois was. It was all business and I think I just wanted to remember it like it was before I left when I was a kid.

My mom was so happy to have me back, but she also wanted me to have a plan. A job or college was my two choices. She didn't care how much I made or where I worked, but I had to pick something. She never wanted rent or help with any bills, but she wanted me to be responsible and be able to fend for myself. Her favorite saying was "I need to know that if I left this earth today you would be ok". Ugh all I wanted to do was come home and be free. This can't be the same grown up I wanted to be because babayyy this is ghetto! I ended up getting a job at Target in no time. I liked getting a check but hated working. I met some awesome friends there, some that I still talk to 'til this day. I knew that $8 an hour would not be the end goal, especially for all the work they required. Back when I was in high school, I took the ASVAB to get out of class one day and I did exceptionally well on it. I had no intention of joining the military at all at that time but now it was a real possibility. The recruiters continued to call me and inquire about my plans but at the time I didn't have a real answer. The Air Force tracked me down and assigned a recruiter to me. One day while I was working a shift, they wanted us to work late into the night and I was not for the foolery. I called my mom and advised I was off and told her she could come to get me. I left that night with no intention of coming back. I told my mom I had decided to join the Air Force and she couldn't be happier.

A blind man could see I chose the Air Force for independence but also, so I didn't have to work at Target anymore. I met my designated recruiter and went to the Military Entrance Processing Station (MEPS) for an evaluation and delayed entry into the program. You go to MEPS to make sure you qualify to join the military. They check height, weight, vision, and everything in between. I was qualified for everything but weight, I told yall I was big. I was now 5"11, 180 pounds. I needed to be less than 169 pounds for my weight. That was a killer to my self-esteem. Even when trying to do right I couldn't. My bonus dad worked with me on diet and exercise religiously. If I was only eating baked food, then so was he. If I had to run 3 miles, then so was he. He was my rider and honestly my rock because without him there is no way I would've been able to make weight. November 28, 2000, I left for basic training. I wanted a fresh start so bad. I wasn't having sex, I was just trying to maintain mental clarity and stay out of trouble and for now, it was working

Basic training was a struggle, but not for the obvious reasons. My Technical Instructor (TI) was cool, and the exercises were easy since I spent the whole summer preparing with my pops. I could handle everything, but the screaming. They belittle you, call you stupid, and just all-around mean. For a youngster that already has esteem issues, it just makes for a bad situation. As I shared before, I had shaky hands and when I was stressed or under pressure they were out of control. The TI's would get together and scream at us while we were carrying our trays and boy did I find out just how much concentration it took for me to not drop my tray or my mandatory 3 waters. I somehow made it through basic training unscathed. I went and saw a doctor once I had graduated from basic training and got diagnosed with essential tremors. ET is very similar to Parkinson's and can get pretty bad with age. There was no treatment back then and nobody really knew much about it outside of the name. This was the absolute last thing I needed! I did what I knew best which was to learn how to control it and pretend like it didn't exist.

I got out of basic training the second week of January 2001. I was now being transferred to my tech school where I learned my trade. I found out I'd be going to Keesler Air Force Base. I was now entering real adulthood. I got assigned a dorm room with a roommate and military life officially began. I was in classes each day to learn my assigned job. We had PT every day and then after that, we were free to roam the base. Eventually, we earned a little freedom which meant we could wear our civilian clothes and leave base. The Navy base was right down the road in Gulfport, MS and well you know what that means. Men, men, and more men. I hung with a few girls, and they all immediately got boyfriends quickly. I hadn't found myself, let alone my own style so it was easy to look past me. My long silky hair was a distant memory. I had decided to do the big chop before that was even a thing. I wore a 2-inch short curly style.

I still got compliments on my hair texture but that was about it. Instead of just dealing with it and loving myself I jumped right into what I knew how to do. Yep, you guessed it, leading with my body. I must say my body was banging. I was the original Meg the Stallion. My waist was small, ass was fat, and my 36C titties were full and perky. I literally was the, it must be ya ass cause it aint ya face, poster child in my head. I could slip on a pair of jeans and tank with no bra and get anyone's attention and I did just that. In typical Kyra fashion, I took it one step further this time. I decided in my head that if I could get someone's boyfriend then not only was I desirable, but I also had something they clearly didn't have. It made me feel special to deal with someone else's man. Gosh, where were my damn morals? Low self-esteem and self-worth ensure you don't have any! I made it a point to only deal with men with a mate. If they had a wife, I felt like I was really winning but I was ok with them just having a girlfriend too. Who raised me, right? To answer your question... my insecurities did, and I was living up to everything they taught me. I was truly a train wreck with no brakes or destination. I had found a way to combat what I considered to be my ugliness and I had used my size to intimidate. I felt like can't nobody check me about their man because I will beat they ass, PERIOD! Somehow, I found no value in having females for friends. I didn't want to be bothered, I didn't want to explain, I just wanted to be…. without question. I always felt like it was a competition as well. In my heart I wanted a female friend but, in my head, I had talked myself out of it for multiple reasons because who wants to be told that they are wrong. Not me!

Luckily, I made it out of tech school alive and in one piece. I was now officially going to be placed for my permanent duty station. I had put in to go overseas, but got Moody AFB in Valdosta, GA instead. Somehow, I ended up right back where I started my adult journey. I was 3.5 hours away from Atlanta and I could visit anytime I wanted to. I arrived at Moody in March and got settled in. I was working 6 days on and 6 days off. Literally, the perfect schedule. I had my own dorm room that was pretty much a studio apartment on base and my own money. Life was great. I was drinking daily, hanging out, and not taking my military career as serious as I should have been. Now that I think of it, I didn't take too much of anything seriously. I didn't have a plan for anything. I was just winging it and by 'it', I mean life. I was depressed and going through the motions. I had met two amazing friends that didn't judge me and didn't care what I looked like. They were genuine and loyal and just what I needed. I was able to get in a routine and just be ok with being me. Without John and Kisha I honestly don't know if I would have made it through that year. We laughed, cried, got familiar with one another's families, and just created our own family dynamic with one another. They knew all my secrets, or so they thought. I never shared my demons with anyone. I was so good at internalizing my shit, that sometimes I even forgot it was there until I was triggered. Things were going so well. I had a few flings here and there with men not worth mentioning. The encounters were like top secret missions. I would go over and slide out before anyone knew I was missing. I would go to my room and shower as if nothing happened. While showering I would sob and just mentally tear myself down. No one really wanted to live this sad life of just being good enough for sex. Everybody wanted to feel important to someone. Sometimes I could walk past the guy I was just with, and he wouldn't even look my way, as if he had no idea who I was. I decided that not only was this counterproductive to my self-esteem, but it was also not a healthy behavior. I began to see that I was doing more harm than good, even if I tried to pretend it was just me having fun. I was done with men for a while. I needed a breather. From that moment, I decided I'd leave that heaux life behind me and focus on getting myself mentally healthy. I didn't have a plan, I told you I wasn't a planner. At that point the idea was just that, an idea. My follow-through has never been one of my strong suits.

I swear every time I'm comfortable, inconvenience bombs are dropped in my life. I get a call to my first shirts office advising that I had been selected for deployment. I had only been on base for 2 months and boom I was going overseas. I was selected to do a deployment to Kuwait. The only thing I remember thinking was, staying late at Target to stock shelves didn't seem so bad. I called my mom and broke the news to her, and she remained calm reminding me that I would be fine. I arrived in Kuwait in May. I was only supposed to be there for 30 days and that turned into months. I shockingly was having a blast. Kuwait was beautiful, definitely not like what you see on TV. I shopped so much, and I ate even more than I shopped. Everything we have in the US they had that, plus some in Kuwait. The people were beautiful. The women had this dark skin, long dark silky hair, and bright eyes. Hell, I was almost lesbian but didn't want to be beat to death, because who has time for that? Nobody! They were living like kings and queens. It definitely opened my eyes to how untraveled I was, and I promised one day I would come back minus the military.

We didn't have our own personal cell phones or laptops, but we had a communications tent. I was sitting in the tent talking to my coworker back in the states when suddenly, she advises me that the World Trade Center had a plane fly into it, and then a second one. I'm going to be honest. I had no idea what the World Trade Center was, but I knew it was bad. The phones disconnected and I immediately heard the alarm going off on base. We were instructed to go directly to our designated bunkers and sit. We were in a full lockdown due to 9/11, and I was in the thick of it. We had practiced this during warrior week but honestly, nothing could compare to living it in real life. I was terrified and alone. I was walking the base with a loaded M16A and a 9mm. I wasn't built for this and just wanted to go home. I cried myself to sleep on a couple of nights. I was lost and going through the motions. I had no communication from the outside world. One day I was sitting in our TV tent and my base commander came personally to get me. He got me in his office and said he needed me to swear I would keep what we were going to talk about between us. I agreed. My mom...my damn mama yall... had somehow got through to our closed base and demanded to speak to me so she could know I was ok. They declined her request and she promised she would be on the first thing smoking to Kuwait if they did not allow her to hear my voice. She got their attention, and I was able to hear my mother's voice. She assured me I'd be ok, and she also assured me if shit went left, she would come find Bin Laden her damn self. After a while, the base calmed down and I was able to leave that joint just in time to get my simple ass pregnant the next month. Lordt, cannot make this shit up.

I had made it through a wartime situation. I had Operation Iraqi Freedom and Operation Enduring Freedom under my belt. Screw everybody who told me I'd be fine enlisting because the chances of me getting deployed or going to war was slim because I did both.

I had made it back to Valdosta and was finally able to sleep in my bed in my dorm. The next morning, I woke up to music playing outside my window. I came out and stood in front of my 2nd floor apartment door and saw a black guy across the courtyard in the next building look my way and smile. I turned around and looked behind me because there was no way he was talking to me, but no one was there. He was absolutely waving to me. He proceeded down his stairs and walked to his green Lumina. He asked my name, and I yelled down and told him. He eventually drove off and I went in the house. I needed to process what just happened. Was he just being cordial? Was he showing interest? Did he notice how Big, Black, and Ugly I was, and his parents just taught him how to be compassionate? I was literally perplexed but went on about my day because I didn't want to get my hopes up. Why did I even care?

Didn't I say I was done and moving on with some sort of self-healing that didn't include men? At this point, this shit must be a real mental illness. Anyway, he had my undivided attention, and I couldn't wait to see him again in passing. The opportunity to see him came back around that night. He pulled up and we spoke briefly, exchanging numbers. He worked in IT, and I worked in the command post tracking aircrew and aircraft around the world. We talked daily and got close within a few days. I kind of liked him. Sadly, if I would've known the devil joined the Air Force, I would have joined the damn Marines.

I felt like I was thriving for once in my life. Even with me finally being in a good spot, I had the desire to go see my biological father. Maybe it was because I was so close to him. Maybe it was because I was feeling a little homesick and needed a little piece of home. I booked a ticket to Atlanta on the Greyhound and let him know I was coming. I initially vowed to myself I wouldn't reach out anymore because he didn't even bother to come to my basic training graduation. Thinking back, he never celebrated me and my accomplishments, even if there weren't that many to celebrate. When I got there, the warm fuzzy feeling I desired didn't exist. I would've been better off just seeing my friends there but it was a lesson learned. It was hard venting to anyone about him because everyone that knew my father loved him. The church, his business partners, and his friends all loved him. My mom always listened, but she wanted me to see for myself and I never was able to. She was so tired of seeing me hurt so any time I discussed it with her she would tell me to let it go, but I never could. Luckily the trip was short and just like that it was time for me to leave. I felt trapped in my own thoughts on that bus ride home. I just couldn't be happy, EVER. I couldn't help but think there had to be something wrong with me, I was the problem. I gave love to everyone but could never get real love back unless it was from my mom.

I made it back to base and carried on with my regular activities. Work was going well, my friendships were thriving, and I was able to quiet the self-talk momentarily. I was spending time with the new guy and of course, we started having sex almost immediately. We will call him D. I was smitten with him, and the best part was he liked me for me. Funny thing is, I couldn't even begin to name a time we went on a date. We would talk and have sex, but this was different. He was into me, and I was into him but for me that wasn't enough. I had met a guy in finance/payroll department, that also showed a good bit of interest in me before I left for my deployment. OMG.... guys are really liking me, and you would think that would whip me into shape, but it didn't. I was still out bumping my head and taking the same tests repeatedly. Mind you I was failing miserably. Everything that I had desired regarding the opposite sex I was receiving but it wasn't enough. So, what in the hell did I really want? Did I even know? I felt like a mouse chasing its tail.

Right after I got into my rhythm of being back on base, I got sick. I mean extremely sick. I couldn't hold anything down. I was tired all the time and I was miserable. My friend told me to take a pregnancy test. I was sure I wasn't pregnant, so I said hell no. I just knew this would pass, and I'd be back and better than ever by the time my birthday came in a few days. My birthday came around and anybody that knows me knows that birthdays are top priority for me. I had big plans, and I was going to bring in my birthday with a good old-fashioned turn-up! November 8, 2001, came around and I was not ok. I got up and sat on the edge of the bed, my head was spinning. I Immediately ran to the bathroom and started vomiting and heaving. I mean my body was jerking and I was sweating. This mysterious illness had been going on a full week, so I went ahead and took a pregnancy test. As soon as the pee hit the stick it changed to PREGNANT. I was mortified. I was defeated and literally ready to just end it all because, obviously, I couldn't get things right in my life. If there was a screwup to be made you can count on me to make it. I didn't have a plan for my own life, how in the fuck was I supposed to become a parent. I didn't even have a license, let alone a car to get myself back and forth to appointments. Luckily since I had been back, I had only had sex with D. I told him and shockingly he was excited, but there was just one problem. D had gotten orders to McGuire AFB in New Jersey, and he was leaving. I was alone and not only was I alone, but I was also pregnant. My life had changed in a matter of weeks.

D had moved to Jersey and well, life kind of just went on. I got sicker by the day and regular activities were a struggle. I called my parents and broke the news to them. My mom sounded ok, but I knew she was probably disappointed. I called my father and he said he would help me get a car by co-signing. I probably should tell you that my father was wealthy. Per his book, he was doing well for himself by that time. In my father's mind based on what he told others is, that I was angry because he wouldn't give me money. Let's be clear, my behavior was trash, but I never wanted his money. I WANTED HIM! As I am getting bigger, I had to move out of the base dorms and into an apartment with a roommate. I couldn't help to think that I should've been living this experience as a young adult not as a young teen mom. I was fighting through the urge to fall into a depression. I flew into Chicago to get my license and have my parents help me look for a car. Everything was set because my biological dad was going to help me. I didn't know the first thing about credit, a down payment, or anything like that. My mother and pops had just learned and got their credit together, so I was on a learning curve. I was severely behind on things I should've known especially when it came to finances and purchases. I get to my moms and we're going to shop for cars. I call my dad, and he starts talking and proceeds to tell me that the holy spirit told him not to co-sign. The darn holy spirit yall! I was crushed and I didn't understand what the fuck had just happened. My mom and pops had just purchased a house and a new car so they couldn't co-sign for me at the time. Needless to say, I went back to Valdosta, and as soon as I landed my mom called me. She explained that they had found a work around and would be able to co-sign for me. She advised me to go to a car dealership where I found the car that I wanted and when I get there to call her. I went and saw a 2001 gold Nissan Altima. They overnighted the paperwork to my mom and the next day she signed it and sent it back. I drove off the lot in a brand-new car, and one less headache thanks to my mom and pops. The thing about my mom is that she will go against the devil in hell for her children. My pops didn't birth me, but he is my rider. I don't know what I would do without him. My pops loved me even when I wasn't loveable and that right there is rare to have from a parent that didn't birth you. I was out in the street using my biological dad as a blueprint when looking for men when I should have been using my pops. Had I of done that, life would've been so much better for me. I always knew that the bond between a dad and a daughter was supposed to be strong, but what I didn't know is that the dad didn't have to be biological. Everything I was searching for I had in my pops, and I just didn't realize it.

My pregnancy was progressing and outside of morning sickness, I didn't have any real complications. I went for my 6-month ultrasound and baby let me just say, God has a sense of humor lol. The nurse said have you thought of NAMES for your BABIES. I asked her who she was talking to. She laughed and said, "you still haven't embraced the idea of twins huh"? I had three ultrasounds previously and there was only one baby so how could this happen to me. I gotta be dreaming right? Who the fuck would give me two babies to parent? I couldn't even take care of me. After the initial shock went away, I got my mom on the phone. I had to call her at work. We talked often when I was off, so me calling her work phone was nothing new. She answered the phone in her work whisper voice. I said to her in a shaky uncertain voice, "Mom, they said I'm having twins." She said, "Girl, get off my phone and quit playing, I'm at work." My mom thought I was joking so she disconnected the phone. I called her back and she knew I was serious. She wasn't panicked though, well maybe she just didn't want me to know. My mom had taken care of me since a baby, so I am sure she knew I had no business with a baby. My mom kicked into overdrive. Everything I needed for those babies she sent priority mail. I mean anything that could fit in a box she sent. The twins had everything they needed between my mom sending things, and my job hosting a baby shower for me. My job got everything my mom didn't send which wasn't much.

I found out that D was dealing with another lady in New Jersey, so we weren't on good terms honestly. Anything I needed came from my parents, and D was just living for the moment when we spoke, but no contributions. Any advice or help I got came from my parents and my co-workers. D was pretty much just the reason I was pregnant, nothing more and nothing less. I should have known procreating with him was a horrible idea, but I wasn't really used to using my thinking cap back then.

June 6th, I woke up with a massive headache. I was scheduled to work an overnight shift that night. My roommate was also my senior controller at work, so she told me to stay home. She said she had a dentist appointment that morning after work and then she would come right home and check on me. I woke up in the middle of the night and drove to Walmart for Tylenol. I laid down and tried to sleep through the night. I knew I had a doctor's appointment that next day on June 7th, so I would let my doctor know. I called my mom that next morning and she told me that something didn't seem right, and I needed to call my doctor. I reached out to my doctor's office at 8am as soon as they opened. I told her my symptoms and she told me I would be fine until my appointment at 3:30pm. I called my mom back and relayed what the doctor had just told me. I begin to cry, and she said "Sha'Kyra call them back now." I get ready to pick up the phone and my roommate comes in and says, "My dentist appointment got canceled." I don't think she even finished saying canceled before I blacked out.

I woke up and my mother was there. I had been out for a few days, so everything was a blur. I was so confused. Was I dreaming, Lord? My mom didn't travel much so to see her face was amazing and scary at the same time. I kept asking what happened and when I got my answer I was floored. I was told that I had passed out and had a few seizures right as my roommate was coming in the door. She immediately called 911 to our apartment. They came in and gave me an IV and tried to get me stable. They got me on the gurney and proceeded to carry me down the stairs. We lived on the top floor. As the paramedics got me halfway down the stairs, I started seizing again so they had to take me back upstairs. I somehow pulled the IV and they had to start over. Once they got me to the hospital they started an emergency c-section where I coded and continued to have seizures. The doctor had the nurse call my mom because she was my emergency contact. They told her that I was likely not going to make it because my heart kept stopping. They told her to get there immediately because someone would have to take the babies. Yall know my mom is about that life so sis, with her non traveling ass, was on the first plane smoking to see about her firstborn. I couldn't see my babies right then because I was weak and in and out of consciousness. I remember thinking to myself, as many times as I wanted to die, I am so happy I didn't. I promised I would never wish I was dead again, but yall know how long my promises hold up. I get cleared to go home and so did my babies. I had them 7 weeks early, but they were perfect. JaMaiya was born on June 7 at 12:58pm, weighing 4 pounds 15 ounces. JaDarhi was born 1 minute after, and he weighed 5 pounds 11 ounces. I remember seeing them and falling right in love. I don't think it hit me how important of a job I'd been tasked with. I remember talking to D right before I get discharged from the hospital and would you believe he had the broad on the phone with him to check and see if I was ok. Chile, when I say I was floored. So floored that I am rolling my eyes now. Come on man who fucking raised this dude?

As I make it home, I feel so welcomed because my mom was there! She had cleaned and washed for me. She had organized and just made my apartment feel like home. My stepmother came for a visit at the same time, and she was great as well. If there is any inclination of how detached my father was from fatherhood, here's some insight. I literally had a doctor call and say, your daughter isn't going to make it. He didn't show up at the hospital that day. He didn't even make it that week. He sent his wife and then he rode his motorcycle down later the next week. I did tell you that I was bare

ly 3.5 hours away, right? My mother lived in Chicago, he was a hop, skip, and a jump away. He was so wealthy he could've caught a flight the same day just like my working mother did. He stayed for a day and then made his way back to Atlanta. Luckily, I was still a passive little girl that was in physical pain, so I let it go. D eventually came to see me and the kids. He stayed for two weeks, and he helped out a lot. He loved the twins, and I could see that clearly.

The commotion calmed down and the visitors did too, my mom sadly had to go back home, and I was left with my roommate and D to help me figure out how to be a mom. D was preparing to leave for NJ, and I can't lie, I was sad. He told me that he wanted us to live in NJ with him so we should get married and put in the request.

Of course, my simple ass went against everything I knew and said OK. I knew damn well I wasn't ready to marry at 20 years old. I figured this would be the only option I had, as far as marriage. It's amazing what low self-esteem and lack of self-worth will make you do. I needed this, I needed to have a man that liked me even if it was because of the twins. I never thought in a million years that I was marrying someone that would eventually turn my life upside down.

Yes, I took my dumb ass to NJ to visit and yes, to get married. I flew back home to GA and put in for my orders. My heart was broken because I was leaving my tribe and the new guy that was smashing my back out. I mean this dude had his girlfriend call my phone while I was dying in the hospital. Yes, I wanted him, but only because I thought no one else wanted me. The guy from finance came and called daily to check on me. He was interested and he made it clear. He came to my house daily and begged me not to move. He even offered to take care of my babies. I considered it and should've gone with my first mind. I was damaged and it was slowly slipping out. Skeletons always show their ugly bones, but I didn't care. I had to go back to work until I got my orders to NJ. I was smashing the guy from finance daily all while trying to prepare for my move to NJ. My last night there, the guy from finance came over and begged me not to leave. I didn't have the heart to risk losing the life I was pretending I wanted. I packed my bags, said my goodbyes, and D came and drove us in my car to NJ. That chapter was closed, or so I thought.

We got settled in our 2-bedroom apartment in NJ and I immediately regretted it. I stuck it out because of course I was thinking I had no other options. I fell into a routine that included work and depression. I wasn't even parenting, honestly. I obsessed about going back to Moody AFB. At that point everything I did was based on my need to be wanted. The idea that a man liked me for me and not because kids or sex was intriguing. I had met D's family and friends, so he was trying to make me feel welcomed, but I wanted no parts. I was communicating with the guy from finance at work anytime I could. D worked in the IT department, and he installed some sort of bug on my work email that sent him every email I sent and received. He discovered everything about my adulterous activities. He was devastated, but eventually, he got over it and we proceeded on with our marriage. I secretly wanted him to be done because I just no longer had the desire to participate. I volunteered for a deployment just so I didn't have to be active in my marriage. Once the deployment was over, I decided I would get out the military. We both did because then we could move home to my hometown and work on us or at least that's what he thought.

We got to Chicago, and I couldn't be more relieved. We moved into our apartment and started working. My mom and pops furnished our whole new apartment before we even made it to the state. We were barely making it financially. I still hadn't figured out how to be a mom. They say it comes naturally, but I must've missed the download of instructions. I am going through the motions at this point. We are always borrowing money from my parents. Our car gets repossessed, and he wants me to borrow my mom's car. We had previously traded the car my mom cosigned on to get it out of her name, and we got a new car. When that car got repossessed and I was forced yet again to reach out to my mom for some help, I was done. I didn't know much about relationships and roles, but I damn sure knew a man will make a way out of no way even if it meant a second job. I no longer cared about his feelings. I had a guy I was dealing with, and I would invite him to our apartment to hang out. I was totally disrespectful, and for some reason, I didn't care. You would think that since I knew what it felt like to be disrespected, I'd be more kind but that was not the case! Somehow it was easy for me to discard people once I was done. D found out and told me I could cheat on him just don't leave him. That gave me the wakeup call I needed. I woke up the next morning and called my mom to advise her I was getting a divorce. That same day I was approved for an apartment, and I moved out. I just knew this would be the fresh start I needed. In case you didn't notice, fresh starts were my thing but when you are the problem there is no fresh start only a new setting with old bullshit.

I moved out and immediately started living my crack head life minus the crack, of course. I was in the streets. I was doing all the undesirable things your parents probably told you not to do. I partied every weekend. I was absolutely living my best worst life, with no regard to anything or anyone. I had become a bulldozer with tunnel vision. If it was in my way, I was plowing right over it. I made sure my kids were clothed and fed, and then it was off to the ratchet life. Their dad lived 15 minutes from me. I had them through the week, and he had them on the weekends. I was doing my thing and finally living the single life I had so desired while being married. I never looked my finance friend up because truth be told, I wasn't really into him back then. I fully believe that it was the chase, and the idea that another person wanted me besides my baby daddy intrigued me.

My kids father begged me to come back home but I refused. I was not in the headspace to deal with it. I didn't file for divorce, but I did behave as though I did. In my head we weren't separated, we were just done. To me separated means away from each other and possibly getting back together, and reconciliation wasn't an option ever. Just as much as I was oblivious to the world of dating, I was just as much oblivious about divorce. I couldn't tell you the first step to getting a divorce or even starting the process. I really didn't even care to try and figure it out. I knew I was done, and having, or not having a divorce couldn't change that for me. I was finally living the life I thought I wanted and well… couldn't shit change that.

Remember how I told you I used to only want men with girlfriends? Yup, I was back at it again. I think for a set of different reasons though or maybe it was a combo deal. I had just got out of a marriage and the last thing I wanted was a relationship. I figured it would be easier to deal with a man with a wife or girlfriend because they can't possibly want a relationship. And of course, that means that my ugly ass was better than their wives. I had changed the type of guys I was interested in and moved on to troublemakers and what parents call, "Thugs". I was juggling two guys at the time, and both had something different I liked. The first one was a big-time drug dealer and the other was a loose cannon that was always involved in something that involved the police. I spent a lot of time with the drug dealer and things were going well. I noticed things were changing between us. He now started to get angry with me when he would see me out. Later, I found out that he and his wife were getting divorced. I recall the time I spent the night at his home. He got up and cooked me breakfast. I ate while he was getting ready for church…smh the irony. I'm getting dressed to go home and as I'm leaving out the door, he runs and slams it and tells me to sit down because I probably wouldn't be going anywhere for a while. He explained that his wife is outside, and she had a gun. She kept calling his phone telling him to tell me to come down so she could "just" talk to me. I don't know if you have ever gone to talk to someone, but you don't take a gun to have the convo. I was shook! I played Billy bad ass in my spare time but today, nope, I don't do gunplay. I will fight anybody moving, but I knew this time was different, so I was scared. He assured me that she would eventually leave and then I could leave. That was at 8am, I ended up leaving around 9pm that night and that's only because the police was outside responding to another call across the street. Lucky for me she was gone, and she didn't get a chance to see my face. I promised I would never do anything like that again…. until the next week came, and I was back over. I was down for many reckless things but dying over them wasn't an option for me. I eventually moved on and started creating this forbidden romance with my loose cannon. If I hadn't learned anything else, I learned I loved to date devils. I was scared but not scared straight though. Hell was very appealing to me for whatever reason.

Spring of 2006 came around and this would be just about the time my mom started to question my sanity, and my soberness. Hell looking back, I am trying to make sure I didn't miss a chapter that involved me doing drugs, lol. I had started dealing with the loose cannon, we will call him P, more often. I recall a time, he called me and asked me to come pick him up. I dropped everything I was doing and made a beeline to Evergreen apartments at his instruction. He told me to wait outside when I got there. I pulled around the back of the building where I could see his girlfriend's apartment and parked. I saw lights flickering through the window and I see commotion, but I don't move. He comes outside and he has a few scratches on his face and he gets in my car breathing hard. He begins to tell me that something happened to his drugs at her house, and he flipped out. He confronted her and they began to fight. I recall him saying "I punched the shit out of her because she was trying to fight me." To a normal person that would have been a red flag, but for me in my simple mind, I felt like he needed me. He must have called me because he could trust me. He ran over me like you wouldn't believe. He didn't call unless he needed something and like a dummy, I was always at his disposal. I was blinded by dick and disruptiveness. He didn't follow the rules by any means. If he was supposed to go left, he went right. My life was being disrupted by his ability to make me forget common sense. I mean and that wasn't a hard task because as you've seen common sense wasn't so common for me.

Time was passing and we had gotten so close. He was always in trouble, but I didn't care. I remember going out to a club one night and we had an amazing time. It was just me and my girl. We partied until the club closed. As we were getting ready to leave, we noticed there was a commotion out in the parking lot. I recognized the faces and saw that P and his brother was amongst those fighting. I saw that as he was fighting the police, there were girls jumping on his back as well. Of course,

I couldn't mind my own business and get in my car and go home, I had to help. I go and I'm pushing the police off him all while getting hits in on the girls too. I had officially lost my mind. The more I think about it the more I think somebody had to slip me some sort of drug because I couldn't be this dumb while being sober, could I?

Summer had come along, and I was working for a major fuel company, but blowing through my money left and right. P had money as well but let's be honest, we didn't have that sort of relationship. I have always been an independent person, so I knew how to get a bag. I wanted to be able to be in the streets every chance I got. So, I quit my job and started relying on my GI Bill which wasn't enough for anything extra other than paying rent. Somehow, I learned that I could write a check from one bank and put it in another account at another bank and take the money out. I began to open multiple checking accounts at different banks for that purpose solely. I was pulling in thousands monthly by doing this. I had so many accounts I couldn't keep up with where I needed to withdraw next. I never even considered the fact that I could go to jail. The money was flowing, and I became addicted. The more money I made the more money I spent. Although I was bringing in a lot of money, I had nothing to show for it. My rent was past due, I was kiting checks to pay utilities from bogus accounts, and I was barely surviving. I was buying everybody everything. I was the "it" girl and I was loving it. I got this bright idea to pull a friend into my schemes when I could no longer get accounts in my name. She had a credit union that she was established with, so I put her on game, and told her she could make extra money. We had a plan and it worked. She made the deposit with one of my checks and it cleared for two thousand. She didn't have a car, so I went and picked her up and we went to the bank. She took some out of the ATM and then had to go in bank because her debit card had a limit on withdrawals. When she went in, she was gone for a while, so I assumed it was just packed. When she came back out, she said the police were waiting for her when she got to the teller. She explained they said she would need to pay the money back and they let her go. I was shook, but not shook enough to give the money back. She ended up getting on a payment plan so she wouldn't have to answer to a judge. I didn't know anybody else who could do it and I was all out of cash. Instead of looking for work I decided to do what I did when things got tough. I ran! I convinced P and my friend that it would be smart to move to the A. P was running from his own shit, so it was easy to convince him. My homegirl needed a little more convincing, but she eventually agreed. The twins stayed with their dad while I got myself situated in Atlanta. P came later once he got everything done that he needed to do. I didn't tell anybody, not even my mother that I was leaving. When I called her in August to tell her, I was already in Atlanta.

I am sure you are probably wondering where I moved to since I was strapped for cash. Well, my biological father came through and allowed me to live at one of his properties. I can't lie, I felt honored because I felt like he cared. He had given me a whole home to live in. The joy was short-lived though. He wanted me to get a job and pay rent. Getting a job and paying rent wasn't an issue, but for him, I refused because I felt like he owed me. I didn't think he owed me money, I felt like he owed me the same treatment that he gave his second-born daughter. I felt like since I was grown, the least he could do was provide housing. I mean he hadn't done anything else. To be completely honest, I was still bitter over him offering a car and then telling me the holy spirit told him not to co-sign for me. So, in every way that I could hurt him, I would, or at least I tried.

My homegirl was homesick and decided she would be going back to Chicago. P was on his way to Atlanta that same week, so I was alone. I had started taking courses again so I could live off my GI Bill. When P got there, I fell extremely ill. I couldn't hold anything down and I was just all around exhausted. Since I had been down this road before, I knew it meant that I was pregnant. I didn't have the heart to tell him though, so I acted as though I was just sick and needed to see a doctor. We went to the emergency room and just as I suspected, I was pregnant. FUCK! I am not even a good mom to the first children I had, and now here I am again about to birth a new baby. P wasn't happy nor sad… he was just kind of impartial. Living with someone and occasionally sleeping with someone is night and day. I liked the sex, but I didn't like him. We didn't even have anything in common. I could feel the depression creeping back into my life. I didn't cook, clean, or anything after I found out I was pregnant. Mostly because I was so sick, but also because I hated my life.

P came and got a job at a car shop, so he was footing the bill for everything. I was set to deliver soon, and I just couldn't get my emotions together. My father was harping on me, my mom thought I should come back home, and me...I just wanted to be dead. I was so stressed throughout my pregnancy, that I was losing weight. My chest was sunk in, and I was frail. I was 199 pounds when I moved to Atlanta but was barely maintaining 160 while 7 months pregnant. I was a mess. One thing I can say that brought light to my eyes was packages from my mom. My baby girl had any and everything she needed. My mom went above and beyond for her grands. The only thing I needed was a car seat and I had been asking P to get one for weeks. I was almost 8 months and knew that at any time I could go into labor.

My ex-husband had moved from Chicago back to his hometown in Maryland. He was set to bring the twins back to me so they could start school there with me. He had no idea I was pregnant and since I couldn't hide it, he found out when he dropped them off. He didn't say much, but I could tell he was devastated, and I honestly didn't care. I even asked him to take me to go pick up a car seat since I still hadn't had one and he did. My mother asked me was anything else left to get and I told her a car seat. She sent me money without me having to ask. I used that money to get the car seat, so I could have one less stress and that is when things got real for me. P was so angry that I had rode with my ex to get HIS baby a car seat. He accused me of sleeping with him and he now believed that our baby was not his. He yelled and called me every name imaginable. I had never seen this side of him honestly, but I instantly recalled the time when I went to pick him up after he had beat his girlfriend up. I won't say I was necessarily scared because he had never hit me or anything, but I was concerned. That issue eventually blew over and we moved forward like the issue didn't exist. I was miserable but worked up some excitement because I knew my baby girl would be making an entrance into the world soon.

July 14, 2007, Destyni Monet' made her arrival. I delivered her 2 weeks early due to me having toxemia just like I did with my last pregnancy. I had a c-section, and I was out of it. P stayed at the hospital for a few hours but left until it was time for me to be discharged. A few days after I made it home things changed drastically. He was angry all the time, he wanted to argue, and he was always in my face. I was standing outside on the porch getting air one evening when I saw the monster in him. He had pulled up and asked me what I was doing outside. We had a new black guy that purchased the house next door, and he swore I was cheating with him. We argued about that, and he grabbed me by my throat and began to squeeze. He told me he would fuck me up. He yanked my hair so hard, I felt like my neck would snap off. I was trying to hold it together, and not cry. I pulled away and moved his arm while trying to pull my baby closer so she wouldn't fall out of my hands. I was terrified. As I am attempting to push him away, he spit in my face and walked in the house. I was already damaged, but that action alone killed my spirit. I went in my room and put the baby down and went in the bathroom and secretly cried. He beat on the door and was like "I know yo ass ain't in there crying." We argued almost daily. I couldn't do anything right in his eyes and I didn't want to. I just wanted him to leave. My twins were in the house when it happened, so they didn't have to see the disturbance outside.

For some people the initial incident of domestic abuse would be enough for them to leave, but for me it wasn't. Maybe I deserved this, maybe this was my karma, or maybe ugly people just don't deserve that fairytale love. I didn't know why, but I stuck around because it had to get better, right? Wrong! Things would be ok for a while and then all hell would break loose. One night we had been arguing back and forth. He was outside and I went to the door to say something to him and of course, we started arguing again. He said something like "Fuck your momma" and I responded with "Fuck yours." That sent him off. He yelled "Bitch, I will kill you" and started heading for the door. He didn't have a key, so I hurried and locked the front door. I ran upstairs to the kitchen, grabbed a kitchen chair, and put it up to my bedroom door so he couldn't get in. I was hoping he would just go away but he didn't. I tried to be calm for my children because we're all holed up in my room. I turned the TV on as to tune out my fears. P had climbed through the basement window and started yelling up the stairs. He tried to open the door, but of course, I had it wedged shut. He beat on it saying he would make sure I was featured on an episode of Maury about domestic violence. He continued to taunt me saying he would get me out one way or another. Suddenly, the TV and the lights go out. He cut all power from the basement. The kids and I were sitting in the dark as I fought back tears. I had staples in my stomach that I was barely recovering from after giving birth, and I had to deal with this nonsense. I was telling myself that it would be over soon because he was just having a temper tantrum. No sooner had that thought left my mind, I smelt smoke. It was bellowing under my door, and I went into survival mode. I felt the door and it was not hot, but the smoke that was coming in under the door was so thick. I had to decide, and I had to make a decision fast. I was on the second floor of a 2-story home. If I ran out the room, I could allow fire in the room or worst, have to deal with him. Instead of taking that risk, I decided I would have to leave the kids in the room, climb out the window, and call 911 from the neighbor's home. I opened the window and looked around to make sure P wasn't outside waiting because at this point, I didn't know what he was capable of. I gave the twins strict instructions to sit together and NEVER open the door. My twins were almost 6 at the time. I told them I would be back after I got us some help. I slid my body out the window and hung so I could get as close to the ground as I could before I let go. I instantly had regrets because I wasn't sure my kids were completely safe. I got the courage to let go and drop. I was barefoot with just shorts and a shirt on. I bolt next door and plead for help from the neighbors. I knocked and when the gentleman came to the door, I explained I was in trouble, and I needed to use his phone to call the police. He explained that he was scared and refused to let me call from his phone. I was desperate for help. I only had a few seconds to make my next move. I ran across the street to a gas station and was allowed to call for help from their phone. Before I could make it out the store and across the street, P comes running saying "I put the fire out that your son started." He was being so nice it was scary. He said, "You can calm down now I handled it." The police responded, and he took the lead on explaining. The police knew something was off, but I didn't open my mouth. One of the cops pulled me to the side to verify the story and just like a dummy I said yes, his version was correct. When the police left, he flipped out and got in his car and left. I immediately called my father on a payphone and told him what happened. He came but I can't help to think how calm he was. I started thinking if this was my sister would he be so calm? He came to check things out and then made sure we were ok I guess and left.

I had made the decision to be done. In my father's defense, he got me a 1996 Buick Le Sabre to make that trip back home. My mom was waiting with open arms. She couldn't wait to get me back. P had gone to jail for something, and I really don't remember if it was related to the fire or something else. I didn't care because this was the perfect time to get the hell down the road. I packed my bags, loaded up the car, and the kids and I hit the road. The trip back home was bittersweet. I knew my mom had her opinions and would voice them. I had another baby that I could barely take care of. The saddest thing of all was that I missed P. I had in my head

I would be better this go round. I was going to show everyone that I have previously disappointed that I was a changed woman. My kids were watching me, and I got tired of living such a hard life at a young age. I was only 26 years old, and I knew I was running out of chances. I wanted to become a better mother, daughter, sibling, and friend. I needed my mom to know that her help was not in vain, and her advice was not falling on deaf ears. My mom had only a few requests if I would be living in her house. She wanted to me pay into a savings account that she would keep for me, and I did that with no problem. The other request was that I keep the room that the kids and I were sharing clean. The last request was that I keep a job and just be responsible overall. This was just the shot I needed. I had a chance at a fresh start as soon as I got home, and you guessed it, I fumbled the chance.

THE DEVIL CAME TO COLLECT

I got myself together and lived happily ever after.... NOT! The chaos in my life was just getting started. Just when I thought I reached rock bottom and was on my way back up, I realized I was nowhere near the bottom YET. My bottom usually had a nice cushion provided by my mom so when I reached rock bottom for real it literally broke me.

I had started working different jobs, but always would quit because they either required me to actually work or the pay wasn't good. I was still partying, but the only difference was that I had an in-house babysitter. My mom loved her grandkids, so she was always willing to watch them. I had started telling my mom that the kids and I would be spending the night at a friend's house, and we would be back before school and work the following Monday. There was no friends or sleepovers occurring. I was getting on the road from Chicago to Atlanta to go visit P. We would spend the whole weekend together as if nothing traumatic happened in prior months. Do you know how damaged you must be to go entertain someone that said he wanted to kill you? Very damaged! I didn't care though because I had found myself in a pattern where I would fall in love with anybody who gave me an ounce of attention. I thought I loved him, and I thought I could help him. I am not sure what I thought he needed help from, but I now know that it was me that needed the help. I eventually grew tired of this crazy situation-ship and moved on. I moved on until I invited him to come live at my new apartment that I had gotten. Yes, you read that right, your girl got herself an apartment. All the money I had been giving to my mother for rent, she returned to me to go towards things I needed. P didn't help me with anything and now looking back he only came over every now &

then. I'm not sure we were ever connected other than our daughter, but we grew apart even more. I stopped paying my rent to afford my life of partying at my new place and ended up getting evicted. I already had a new place lined up for myself though, so I wasn't worried. History always repeats itself, so I got put out of that one too, it was just an ugly cycle.

I slowly had the desire to pull my life together, so I ended up finding another apartment and a better job at Allstate. I met a young man that really was into me. Like really into me. He took his time to learn me, what I liked, what I didn't like, etc. He spent time a lot of time at my house, and we laughed together. He was patient and he was kind. He was also 20 and I was about 28. I always say GOD sent him so that I could know what real love felt and looked like. He stuck it out with me after I lost two more apartments and my house. Of course, I always had a reason why it happened, so it didn't make me look bad. He lived in hotels with me without a complaint. My car got repossessed and he gave me his car to use. I mean he was heaven sent. My parents and his mom loved one another. We worked together so we saw each other every day. Eventually, he was spending the night at my house every night. He was bonding with my children, and they loved him as well. I was very insecure, and he was much younger, so I always felt like he was cheating. He could go to the bathroom at work too long and I was accusing him of cheating. We started arguing and I would slap him, bust his lip, and send him to work bruised. It was just a really bad situation. We carried on like this from 2010-2012 when eventually he got overwhelmed with all my baggage and anger. He called it quits and I was devastated. I was broken beyond repair. The only man who really loved me no longer loved me. My identity during that period was no longer Sha'Kyra it was "his girlfriend." That was who I was and once it was gone, I was lost. If there was any reason for me to clean my life up, it was him. Now that he was gone there was no point. I had lost focus of elevating and went on a downward spiral. I made the decision I was going to move back to Atlanta, and I started focusing on that. Everything fell into place because the Allstate call center closed, and I got unemployment. Although everything seemed to fall in place it was a gift and a curse, but I wouldn't realize it until it was too late. I went on a girl's trip to Atlanta and made it my mission to find a place. I partied at night and looked for someone who would give me a place with my rental history. Last day came around and someone called me back saying they had a townhouse in Stockbridge. I never saw it in person, only photos, but I took it. I sent my money and set the move-in date for April 15.

I was scheduled to leave on April 13 of 2013. On April 10 I woke up in the middle of the night in severe pain. I could barely walk upright. The pain was overwhelming, so I drove myself to the emergency room at about 2am. I got there and they tested me for STDs, and it came back negative. I also was having back pain that doubled me over. They believed I had a UTI, so they gave me a shot of some medicine called Rocephin. She left to grab my discharge papers and she comes back about 3 minutes later. I tell her I feel like I can't see the TV. She told me to just lay down for a moment and before I knew it, my tongue was swelling, and my vision was gone. I had to run out for help because I knew if I didn't get help, I'd be dead. I can remember so vividly to men in oversized coming to my rescue. One was so tall I can't even begin to guess his height, and he was hovering over the other man. The other man was short, but also had a suit on. I couldn't make out their faces because it was like a light shining on them. I remember thinking to myself I finally got some help. I had passed out and I can remember being picked up and held up by the two men in the suits.

All of this felt so familiar, I had been down this road before. I woke up and my mom was standing there. I was tubed and couldn't speak, but I was so happy to see her face. She always came through whenever I needed her, no matter the time or request. If you recall, I told you I never paid my bills. My mom had told me she was tired of the hospital collections department calling her phone and I needed to remove her as an emergency contact. I told her ok but knew I wouldn't because who else would I list...my bio dad?!? I think the hell not! Had I removed her I would've been in the hospital alone. The doctors told me that there was no way I made it through my throat closing and my heart-stopping. I was literally a miracle for the 3rd time. I forgot to mention my breathing issues. I never had asthma and then I had a severe asthma attack a few years back that almost took me out. I couldn't help but take inventory of all my near-death experiences. I kept thinking that God keeps sparing me, but why? I couldn't figure it out, especially since I was so damaged. I saw no value in myself so how did God keep pulling me from the pits of hell. I felt in my heart I didn't deserve to be spared. I remember laying in that hospital bed questioning life. I would lay and think all night long. I knew that since I was spared, I needed to do better and be better! Before I got discharged, I was speaking with the nurse about the two men in the suits. I described them and what I remembered happening and was told that there were never any men in suits helping. I knew then God had sent help!

The day I was released from the hospital was the day I loaded my U-Haul in preparation to make that long trip to Atlanta from Chicago. One thing about me is once I set my mind to something I see it through and there was no stopping me. I spent the night at my mom and pops the night before I left. I typically have no issue moving away, but this time was different. I was fighting back tears the whole night. I just wanted my mom to know I appreciated her. I needed her to know that everything she had taught me was in me and I was going to bring it out. I wanted to make her proud. I WAS going to make her proud.

I arrived in GA on April 16 with the help of my friends Shannon and Brittany. They drove my kids in my car while I drove the U-Haul. My life was in such shambles, I had to get the U-Haul in someone else's name because my license was suspended. Who knew when you got a ticket you actually had to go to court and answer to your offense? LOL. I got all my furniture moved in and was officially a resident of GA and I vowed this time would be a totally different experience than my last time, but that dream of greatness was of course short-lived. I was way better at just barely making it instead of excelling. The bare minimum was always my go to, and I was ok with that.

Things with D were not good at all. He wasn't present in the twin's life. I had finally got a divorce from him and couldn't be happier. Our co-parenting skills were nonexistent and so was his communication. In an effort to try and be a better person and ex-wife, I attempted to reach out and try and form an alliance. I knew the kid's birthday was coming up and I wanted him to be a part of their 11th birthday. He was receptive and open to the idea. We scheduled it so that he could come, and we could celebrate their birthday together with them. He told me he could pay for a hotel, but we would have to do something at the house since he would be strapped for cash. I just told him he could stay at my townhouse while here and he could sleep in the kid's room. I figured with the money he had saved he could take the kids out and just enjoy the day with them. The day came and D rolled in from Maryland. The kids were in heaven, the smiles were endless. We got along fine, and he stayed in the kids' room with no issue. Scratch that, he smacked my ass and I had to get him together because I was disgusted. Other than that, the visit went just like I imagined. I was hoping that maybe he would start helping me with the twins more than he did. Even before this alliance, I was still putting his name on Christmas gifts and birthday gifts. I needed help, but more than anything I needed the kids to have a great relationship with their father. I didn't want my children to have a relationship with their dad like the one I had with mine. D went back home, and I moved on with my normal routine. I had issues with my townhouse, and I moved out. I must say that my bio dad came through again with offering his house up to the kids and me. We moved in along with my cousin and her children. I again was not paying rent at all. I didn't feel it was necessary. Yes, you read that right. I thought I should be entitled to free rent, smh. I had so much baggage to unpack, and I am not talking about from moving. I had no intention of unpacking it or sorting through it either.

My unemployment had run out and I was no longer getting my GI Bill. I was broken in every sense of the word. We had lights but no water or gas at my father's place. I didn't have the money to get the utilities in my name, so we were using the bathroom at the hospital around the corner from our place. We were using jugs of water to wash up in the sink. I was waiting for one last GI bill payment. Once that came in, I got the utilities on, but it was still a struggle to maintain. I knew I needed a job immediately. I saw that the hospital was hiring for registration, and I applied and got it. I was making $14 an hour and it was listed as a PRN position. PRN just means that it's not full or part-time, but as needed.

Somehow, I lucked up and I got pulled in on full-time hours with benefits. Life was starting to look up, but I was still going out partying like I had no responsibilities. I guess you could say I didn't have responsibilities, since I refused to pay rent.

My cousin had met a guy and moved out with him, so it was just me and the kids. I was working so hard to try and pretend that I was fixed but I had no idea what I was doing. I met a woman named Kiya and she literally changed my life. She was my person. She was my person, but I was also intimidated by her. Kiya had been through a lot, and none of it had held her back from following her dreams. She made a way without excuse. She made me feel like the unobtainable was very obtainable. She was facing struggles and she never let it get her down or make her deviate from the plan. I always admired her and knew one day I would take everything she showed me and apply it to my own life. She had no idea, but I was watching her every move because she was the real deal. The one thing that stood out to me was that she was always so positive even when she had reason to be negative. The things that everybody in my life was trying to tell me.... Kiya somehow showed me instead of telling me and forever I will always be grateful to her. I had also met another young lady on Facebook in a group I was in. Keisha was my fun, free, and stable friend. She reminded me a lot of myself in many ways, but she also reminded me of what I wasn't. She lived a full confident life and when I was with her, I felt like I could be or do anything. She poured into me when she had no idea that I needed it. The nail dates, vent sessions, and just all around hanging out would spark something in me that I didn't even know was in me. I didn't know that God was placing people in my life that I needed both now and, in the future, more than I ever could imagine. Keisha turned out to be more than just the best, she was my family.

I had gotten an amazing shift at the hospital. I was working 3 days on and 4 days off. My twins were 12 and able to stay home while I was working. They all rode the bus home together. I had a plan where if things went left, I was only 3 minutes from my house. My daughter was responsible with my youngest, so I really didn't worry. I was doing the best I could with what I had. I worked from 5am-5pm, Wed-Fri at the hospital. I was finally feeling like I was moving in the right direction. I was still making little to nothing, so I needed help. My water bill was coming due and because I was still financially irresponsible, I didn't have it. I had probably made a payment arrangement and couldn't follow through. I reached out to the twin's father and asked him for help. I never reached out to him for help because I already knew what the answer would be. He hadn't helped in years, so I bit the bullet and reached out. He told me he didn't have it. I was so angry because the kids always had birthday and Christmas presents without his help and I never once let them know he didn't get them anything. I felt like the least he could do was help with the water bill. I was angry so I told him I'd be putting him on child support, and I hung up on him. Time went on and I didn't think much of the blow up we had. I continued to go to work and party. My level of pretending like all was well was expert level. No one besides my mother knew what I was really dealing with, and I preferred to keep it that way.

Summer of 2015 had come around. The kids had begun

to enjoy sleeping in. There was no big routine to be had anymore since school was out. I would just get up and head to work before the sun came up. I always knew I could expect a call around 10am from the kids to let me know they were up and moving around. This particular day was different though. Work was kind of busy so by the time I realized I didn't get the check-in call it was around noon. I called the kids cellphone and got no answer. I assumed that maybe they had slept in so every 10 minutes I would call but wouldn't get an answer. I began to panic so I told my manager I would need to leave if I didn't hear from them in the next few minutes. A couple minutes later, my world would be turned upside down in a way that I was not prepared for.

My phone chimed so I got a sense of relief thinking it was the twins checking in. When I opened my phone what I saw shook me to the core. I am sitting chatting with my manager as I open the picture and I saw my twins in the back seat of a car with their dad's father and the next picture was a picture of the "Welcome to Tennessee" sign. I instantly started sobbing. I couldn't sob much longer because I remembered I had a 7-year-old that was unaccounted for. I began to call the twins phones back-to-back with no answer. Finally, I got a text from their father stating that he had taken Destyni to my father's office and dropped her off. He didn't mention what happened or why though, so I was still in the dark. I couldn't hold it together. I began sobbing and vomiting uncontrollably. I pulled it together long enough to try and process what happened. I got in my car and sped the 10 minutes to my father's office. I got out the car and went in to find my disheveled daughter with mismatched shoes on, too little shorts, and a tank top that was clearly not hers. She had dried up stains on her face and she looked like she was in shock. I asked where the twins were, and my uncle stated that their dad had taken them. I went from confused to violently livid. I had to leave, or I knew I would light a torch to the building with everyone in it. I got to my home and saw that it had been turned upside down. Their father had taken anything of value from my house.... TVs, video games, and anything else he could fit in his vehicle. I got my mother on the phone and she said she would call me back. When she called me back, she said "Sha'Kyra...D has taken the kids and I don't think he is bringing them back." In a matter of two hours, my life went to hell. I may not have been the best mom, but I damn sure loved my kids. I called the police and went and filed a report but was told since we had gotten a divorce without including the children, he had just as much of a right to them as I did. I was by myself on figuring this out.

Imagine not only finding out that your children have been taking, but the person that helped create you was sort of in on it. I couldn't help but think that if D pulled up on my mom and said here's Destyni and I am taking the kids, she would have said "Fuck no" let me call my daughter first. On top of all the manic feelings I was having, I was mostly feeling betrayed. See, my father and I had got into a big fight prior to this, and deep in my heart I knew this was his way of getting me back for not paying rent and not getting out. The person that I wanted to love me so bad betrayed me in a way I'll never be able to get over. He was supposed to protect me by any means but that never would be the case, I guess.

How does one move forward after something like this? I don't think you ever move on; you just learn to cope.

My mom came in clutch as usual. She sent me money to drive my new car that I had just purchased to her house. She knew that not only did I have to figure out how to handle this, but I also would need to return to work which meant I'd need to pay for daycare for Destyni. She would watch Destyni over the summer to help me get my life together. I arrived at her home in Chicago two days later and I was exhausted. I was exhausted from crying, from worrying if my twins were ok, and from the drive of course. She said the skin around my eyes was black and my face was dry and peeling, probably from crying for 3 days straight. I spent a week at my parents' home calling lawyers, calling the twins, and just calling anyone that would hear my cry. I received an email from D that stated, "If I hadn't ruined what we were trying to build when we were married, I wouldn't be going through this." I knew he was bitter but not bitter enough to do this to me. I remember seeing that message and feeling rage but also, I wanted everyone else to see he didn't do this to protect his children, he did it to get back at me. My time at my mom's was coming to an end, and I was mentally fried. I had to get back on the road and head back home ALONE.

Leaving my baby was one of the hardest things I ever had to do, but I had no choice. My leave was coming to an end, and I had to get back to work sooner than later. I made the drive from Chicago to Atlanta and the whole trip I was either crying or trying to figure out how I could run my car into something without harming some innocent person. I replayed the thought in my head repeatedly. I knew that my baby girl was in a safe place, and I was clearly a fuck up, so leaving her behind would help her rather than hurt her was my thought. I remember pulling over to the side of the road and trying to talk myself into getting out and just walking into the traffic on the highway. I couldn't believe I was having these thoughts, but I was. I somehow had convinced myself this was the only way. I opened my car door, and a big semi-truck was coming up in the lane next to the side of the road and I could feel the wind force my door open more. I grabbed the car door and slammed it shut and began to sob uncontrollably. I started my car and got off the highway at the next exit and sobbed until I felt like I was going to vomit. I was eventually able to pull myself together and get back on the road. After a long day, I finally made it back to GA and put on my best "Everything is good" face. I called any attorney or private investigator that would listen to me. I didn't have any money to pay for an attorney, so I had lost hope. D called one day asking could I unenroll the kids at their current school, so that he could get them enrolled in his area. I was floored and was bitter, so I didn't care if they went to school or not. I assumed that if I could hold off on releasing their records then he would be forced to bring them back. The school in GA helped me as best they could but eventually, they had to release them since there was no court order saying that I had primary custody. The last bit of hope to getting them back was gone. I hadn't talked to my kids, seen their faces, or even got acknowledgement that they were ok in God knows how long.

Life took a turn for the worst, and I started to spiral. Prior to this I had gotten my divorce, got a great job, purchased a brand-new car, and I wanted to be better. I wanted to show those that meant the most to me that I could be a good person. Now, I just didn't care about anything. I started calling off work, partying, and drinking often. I fell right back into my old routine because it felt familiar. I contemplated suicide hourly, it just felt right. I had made so many mistakes in my life that maybe this was my payback. Honestly, nothing could be worse than me losing my kids…not even death and I was ok with that too.

OH SHIT I'M THE TOXIC FRIEND

Taking inventory of my life when I was at rock bottom showed me every area I needed to change. I was taking inventory daily, sometimes a couple of times a day. I didn't have the kids, nor did I really have a life, so I had plenty of time to think. I asked, "Why me?", often because I just couldn't understand how I got where I was. There was always lots of thinking and no action with me. I was working a shift at the hospital talking to a patient as I got them registered for their procedure. As I walked them back to the waiting room, I began to feel sick. I got back and sat back in my chair and my heart began racing, my palms were moist, and I felt like I was going to vomit. I ran to the single bathroom and as soon as I locked the door it all came up. It wasn't physical vomit but, it was emotional vomit that wasn't stopping anytime soon. I wept, I sobbed, I prayed, and wept again, for a good 15 minutes. I didn't understand where it was coming from because I was doing so well just existing in all my chaos. I had tricked myself into thinking everything was going to be ok. I mean I knew it wasn't because there was no scam or anything I could pull to fix this. Anybody that knows me knows I hate public bathrooms but this day it didn't matter. I sat down on that floor and cried out silently. I needed help and I needed help bad. All the inventory of my life I had taken had started playing in my head like a movie. I had been through so much stuff that I am surprised I made it this far without a breakdown. A lot of things happened to me in my life that I couldn't control, but I also was the cause of a lot of things as well. "Holy Shit, I was the 'toxic" friend was my thought once I calmed down. I was the poster child for the word toxic. I was toxic to myself and those around me. I ended up leaving work early that day, but I think my life was forever changed in that bathroom.

I didn't immediately become un-toxic of course nor did I want to. I had gone through life blaming every single bad thing on my past and if I couldn't do that anymore then I only had myself to blame. I had learned to use my father as a crutch as to why I was so fucked up and to me, that was easier. I decided instead of fixing my past I'd focus on my future. I still partied and moved the same way, and the only difference was that I was fully aware that what I was doing was not the way to go. I guess I just was not ready, but I had better get ready because my life was about to change.

I slowly began to pick apart my life and I started in the friend category. I was never one to wish bad on any of my friends, but I also never really wanted to see them win. When I was in my early 20s, my life was crap and I remember trying to be around other people who were making the same screw-ups as I was. When you are in the thick of bad decisions the last thing you want is someone holding you accountable. This is no dig on any of my friends from my younger years, I think we all were naïve and immature. I felt comfortable being around people with no goals and no ambitions because I was living life on a prayer and with little effort. I loved being around people that didn't have jobs and didn't have their own place because as sad as it may have been I felt I was better than them. I call it the "at least mentality" because at least I had a job and a place. When I would find people that weren't as bad as me, I'd make them as bad as me. If I was doing check fraud, I showed them how to do it. If I was calling off work, I convinced them to do the same. I ensured I wasn't the only one at the bottom. I didn't care who I drug or kept down there with me. I was the worst type of "friend" you could possibly get. I didn't want anyone to do better or be better than me, but I was ok with them being on the same level though. These behaviors allowed me to walk around damaged and dangerous. The thought of that alone made me sick because I loved my friends, I really did, I just didn't know how to be a friend. I was never dependable unless it meant being on time for a club. I led with money most times because that's all I had to offer. If they were ever hungry, needed an outfit, or help with gas money, I had you. I could provide physical things but emotionally I was unavailable. I was everything I would tell my daughters to avoid when picking a friend. As harsh as that reality was, it was true. I missed so many opportunities in my life to be a better friend because I didn't see the value in myself, so how could I see the value in someone else.

When they say, "friends are a reflection of where you can go," it's so true. This saying revealed why I was so intimidated by Kiya and Keisha. They were everything I felt like I could never be. They also made me dream and I began to dream big. Imagine a life of living but no dreaming! You have nothing to look forward to. I didn't think I was worth dreaming, the thought was toxic AF. It would have been so easy for Kiya and Keisha to be the person I was to my old friends, but they were everything but that, and for that I am appreciative forever for them. You just don't become a crappy friend overnight; it takes time to build that flawed trait and I had 20 plus years to do so. This led me down the rabbit hole of healing.

I started to do the work. I had friends that I interacted with daily, so this was the easiest hurdle for me. Don't get me wrong, it was hard but in comparison to all my other toxic waste, this was easiest. I made the decision that I would start from scratch. I would begin being the friend I wished I had in my childhood. I needed to be the friend that celebrated friends without feeling slighted. I needed to want to see all my friends succeed. I had to hold my friends accountable so they could knock every goal out. I had to change my way of thinking in every aspect of the word. I no longer allowed myself to become slighted because someone else was winning. I have this thing where I expect instant results. I'm trying God so why am I not winning too was my thought process even if it's only been a day of change. I wanted to be better but sometimes doing the work was too much. I began working through it and slowly started to see a change. Before I knew it, I no longer cared about me winning because I got just as much gratification in seeing my FRIENDS win.

Oh, please don't think this was an easy task though. I had a good start to unpacking all this baggage but honestly, I was just taking the issues from one bag and filling up another bag of toxicity. I had learned to unpack the baggage, but no one told me I needed to learn to sort through and discard it. Have you ever gone on a trip and as soon as you got back home you had to fly out for another trip the same day? Do you just take your dirty clothes out of your bag, and put those same dirty clothes in a new bag and fly out? I would hope not because although you changed the bag the clothes are still dirty. The same goes for trauma, bad habits, and unbecoming traits. I took my toxic friend traits out of the friend equation, but I applied them to other aspects in my life. I had to unpack, sort through, and discard what I didn't need anymore. I had to get to the root of why I even had these behaviors and boy did I uncover some ugly truths!

I spent many nights questioning myself and my worth. I had to dig deep and go back to the day in 3rd grade when my crush called me ugly. You see, up until then I was the smart, funny, good grade getting, first pick at everything in class type of kid. As I think back, I gave my power away to a little peasy head little boy that probably was insecure in his own dark skin. The moment I let him shake me was the moment I let him decide my future. In my eyes I was no longer smart, funny, helpful, a joy to be around, or the All Around the World champ...that's a math game for those that don't know. I allowed him to reduce me to a big, black, ugly, and a USELESS little girl. I had to go back and correct all those things I had hated about myself and that was healing in more areas than just the friendship area. I had begun the process of being the un-toxic friend but yall, I was still toxic as hell in so many other areas. I knew that if I wanted to see real change, I had to be all in no matter how hard. Challenge Accepted!

Yall know my father was a soft spot. As much as I was able to place the blame on him for my behavior, 99% of my issue was me. In the words of my mom, I needed better letting go skills. When it came to my dad it was like beating my head against a wall and expecting it to move out your way. I had tried everything to get his love to no avail. I remember one year I had my mom get these Kirk Franklin DVDs and I called to tell him, in hopes that he would see that we had something in common. He was a Christian and loved gospel music and so was I, but that didn't work. I tried to "play nice" and be friends but that didn't work. I even went as far as getting revenge by damaging his home he lent to me and well that didn't work either. My sister was graduating, and I got invited to say a little something at her party. I had written out this heartfelt letter to her that I read in front of everybody. I read my letter fighting back tears, but I got through it. I thought that maybe they would see my efforts and realize I wanted to be a part of the family. It was then time for my father's presentation. He got up and washed her feet and gave her a gift and I couldn't help but feel envy. My father then got up with tears in his eyes to give his speech. Somewhere in the speech he said "if I had to choose a daughter, I'd choose you every time" … my heart was shattered AGAIN. That sadness immediately turned to anger. I was seeing red and if I had gone with my first mind, I would have flipped every fucking table in there over, but instead I walked out. I wasn't in such a good headspace so me flipping the tables wasn't very far-fetched. I started to replay everything that made me hate him…from me not having but one picture in their home down to his church friends saying, "I didn't know you had an older daughter." I felt invisible! I instantly got my mom on the phone, and she was able to talk me down. For years I went through this until it dawned on me that I allowed this treatment. My desire to be wanted so bad, to be loved so much, and to feel like I was part of the family overruled every bit of common sense in my brain. I was so consumed with my desires that I overlooked this toxic behavior as just wanting love. This behavior bled over into every relationship that I had. Because I wanted love so bad, I accepted anything especially when it came to men. I blame me, not for the lack of love, but for the allowance of the subpar treatment as it pertains to my life. I expected a me out of him and that's where I went wrong. Instead of forcing love and forcing a relationship, I knew that I had to either meet him where he was at or leave him where he was at. I had begun to understand that there were going to be people that couldn't give me what I need and that was ok. Them being unavailable was never a reflection of me. I was slowly taking my power back and I must admit this is a hard one that I didn't grasp until 2020. I was no longer pointing fingers unless it was at myself. My dad was a young father and while I wasn't giving him a pass, I also wasn't going to let his shit mix with my shit. I no longer was willing to waste my time trying to get him to see my point of view.

The hardest part was not being bitter while doing it. I am a work in progress, but now I have reclaimed my power and I am in control. The normal things that would send me into a toxic spiral are easier to identify and work through. I can't say it hurts less because it doesn't but coping and moving forward in a positive manner is now doable.

Being big, black, and ugly was a heavy weight to carry as an adolescent and even as a young adult. It made all my decisions for me. It allowed me to excuse bad behavior. It made me a monster almost. It pushed me to be everything but what I was put on this earth to be. Truth is, I didn't even know what I was put on this earth to do or even why. I created counterproductive habits and ideas to help me deal with my issues instead of getting to the root of the issue. I had tricked myself into thinking I couldn't be that UGLY because these men were having sex with me. I flipped being bigger into being an advantage that would make me fight everything moving. If they dissed me, I could just beat them up because I was bigger. And well black, I didn't have a reasoning or defense mechanism for that, so I pretended that I loved it, but anytime I looked in the mirror I cringed in disgust. If someone asked me to pick one thing, I loved about myself, I drew a blank. There was not even one thing I liked about me let alone loved about myself. As I began to reflect on my self-esteem issues it brought me back to every relationship with the opposite sex I'd been in and what I saw wasn't a pretty reflection I saw looking back at me.

Each time I put focus on healing a new area of my life, it felt more traumatic than the previous one. I thought once I dug through my toxic friendship behaviors that everything else would-be smooth sailing. It was devastating to look back and reflect, but I made myself a promise to heal me, so I ripped the Band-Aid off and continued with the process. I reflected on all the men I dated and wondered how and why. The men that I encountered were the perfect reflection of me. Broken, lost, and insecure. I want to say they were able to manipulate me but honestly, I was way too smart for that. I'll just say I allowed them to use me while I was using them for some sort of sick self-gratification. Men were my weak spot since 3rd grade. Everything I did was to get the approval of a man. The gratification that my molester got from molesting me, even though I was ugly (or so I thought), led me to equate that to being desired. He may not have liked me, but he liked doing sexual things to me and I had his attention during that time.

I knew that to heal the part of my life that related to men, I had to deal with my self-hate. I knew that I'd never allow a man to hit me, light my house of fire, berate me, belittle me, or treat me bad in any way if I just valued myself. I was sitting at work one day and I didn't have any patients scheduled to come in, so I was just scrolling Facebook. I saw a post about self-worth. As I said, I was a smart woman, so I knew what the words meant individually, but honestly had not thought about the meaning as a whole. I went to google and saw that it pretty much meant the same as self-esteem. I looked up videos on how to fix self-worth issues and there were so many. I saw a video about standing in the mirror, positive affirmations, and positive self-talk. I made a list of all the things I hated about myself, and boy was that a long list. Each day I started focusing on one thing I hated about myself and where the hate came from. I had given everybody, but myself the opportunity to choose how I felt about myself. I slowly started to see the beauty in myself. My chocolate skin was not a hinderance at all, it was a part of what made me who I was. The melanin is what makes that glow under the sun that much more radiant. My almond shaped eyes were dreamy and exotic. My long torso and legs could make an outfit stand out like you wouldn't believe. My bright white smile could light up the room. My teeth were perfect. I got so in tune with myself that I had to prevent myself from getting cocky. See self-worth has nothing to do with looks most times, but my lack of it was definitely based on my looks and what I thought I lacked. I got up each morning and wrote with lipstick on my mirror, an attribute that I was learning to love. That attribute stayed up until I began to understand the beauty in it. It was difficult because for years I had a picture in my head of who I wanted to be physically, and it was nowhere near who I was in reality. She was 5'5, size 6 shoe, long full curly hair, light skin, and light eyes. I would lay and often dream about what life would be like if I were her. I couldn't help but imagine how much better I would have treated myself. I knew that I would love myself way more if I were her. I had to learn how to say goodbye to her. I had to understand how she, although just an image in my head, hindered me from loving myself. I began to understand how she stunted my growth and I started replacing her attributes with my own. Slowly she began to fade from my thoughts, and before I knew it, she was gone. Once I got past the physical hindrances I worked on my emotional.

In the process of this healing journey, I realized I didn't know me. I didn't know what I liked, what I didn't like, if I liked relationships, if I liked men, or hell if I liked women. I had been going through life with shit coated sunglasses on, stinking up everything I saw so I couldn't appreciate anything. I had to learn who Sha'Kyra was. I knew that everything I did in my past was rooted in insecurity, especially sex. I had a chance to redo everything. I learned to like my own touch, my laugh, my smile, and I started dreaming. I started having goals for myself. I started trying to say yes to more things and some I failed at and guess what.... I didn't die! Failure did not kill me. Why did I feel like I didn't deserve anything good? The answer that stood out was I didn't allow myself the opportunity of a good thing because that meant there was a chance I'd fail. No one told me that failing is sometimes a part of the process and that it was ok. I had walked through life wanting to be invisible and for the first time I was living out loud. I didn't care who had seen my faults or my failures. I knew that with those faults and failures they'd also be getting my wins too. I often downplayed my abilities, so I didn't stand out, but not anymore.

I should probably tell you that I backslid and reverted to my old ways of doing things quite often. I eventually got back on the right track, but I received many good lessons in grace during that time. One of the reasons that living on the wild side was appealing to me was because there were no expectations for myself so there was no way I could let myself down. Everyone else had deemed me a screw up so they didn't expect much either. When I didn't produce anything, no one was concerned or disappointed. I guess you could say I set the bar pretty low. Low bars allowed me to stay stagnant and comfortable in my own chaos. I didn't have to worry about disappointing myself or anyone else. Now that I was on the right path, I was so scared that I'd disappoint people that were rooting for me, and let's be honest, sometimes I did. I felt like everyone was just waiting for me to fail so they could remind me that I was still the same person that constantly failed them. I had to teach myself that self-correction and growth doesn't mean mistakes won't be made, self-correction simply means that you are holding yourself accountable when you do mess up.

I was doing surgery without even being a doctor. I wasn't doing actual surgery, but I was definitely doing a soul surgery. My toxic behaviors created emotional toxins that started to spread from one area of my life to the next. Being toxic is so tricky because by the time I even realized I was toxic I had already made so many bad decisions that there was no quick fix. I had blamed my dad, God, the guy that molested me, my color, and everything else on my bad decisions. I refused to believe that me, the victim, was getting in her own way. I was just playing the cards that were dealt to me, right? The truth was that I had ample opportunities to throw those cards in the nearest trash and create my own cards but being toxic was just easier for me. I hated knowing that a lot of the bad in my life could have been avoided had I just did some soul searching and held myself accountable.

I started really focusing on self-improvement. The one thing that was going to be a huge hurdle was my family dynamic. I had pretty much shut my closest family out. My mom only heard from me when I needed something, and I knew that wasn't right. I had built up so much resentment, that it was hard for me to even have a conversation with any family member. When my children had got taken from me, I blamed everyone. My mom kept in touch with D because she wanted to stay in touch with the kids but to me, I felt like it was a slap in the face. My aunt was friends with him on Facebook and made a point to tell me how he was a good father so I shouldn't be upset so yea, I was hurt. That alone made the calls less and less frequent between my family and me. See, I was always that friend that showed up for my friends no matter right or wrong. I was the friend that was ready to bust a broad head over my friends. I will check a bitch in public about my friends and I'll correct my friends in private. Somehow, I wanted that from my family. I wanted them to show out for me, to let D know he wasn't shit and would never be shit, but instead they forged a relationship for the twins, and I just couldn't wrap my head around that. It felt like betrayal! I felt like they chose him over me, and that was a feeling that even I couldn't express. I felt like the people that I always had in my corner had to choose a side and they didn't choose me. I was very bitter and angry, but I knew that I needed to mend my relationship between my mom and I because if anybody deserved to see me win it was my mom. She loved me even when I was losing, and she was there no matter what. She cursed me out all the time, but I swear I deserved it, lol. She called me on my shit, and I hated it. She was not afraid to correct me when I was wrong. Most importantly, she loved me unconditionally. D had already taken to parts of me and there was no way in hell I would allow him to be the reason that I lost my mom too. I decided not to tell her but show her that I was moving in the right direction, and that she had plenty of reason to be proud of me. It took a while, but I did just that. I made every effort to rid myself of the toxic behaviors because I realized everything, I was building could be dismantled if I didn't.

CHASING MY MONSTERS

Time began to pass, and I continued on my journey to healing. I met a man, and he was like the mirror image of me. He was learning himself all over again after a nasty separation and soon to be divorced as well. He allowed me to be who I was without judgement. I explained to him who I was, that my kids were taken, that my hands shook, and that I was working through all of it. He was not phased and naturally I couldn't help but to be smitten. He became my voice of reason, even if we were just friends at the time. We fell in love and eventually got married, even though we vowed to never make the mistake of marriage again, he was my person. I already wanted to be better, but when I was with him, I wanted to be better than better. He never once judged me and allowed me to be me. We eventually packed up and moved to Arizona. I had made peace with the fact that I was so fucked up in the past that I didn't deserve to have my kids. I made the decision to move forward and do well in life until I could get my hands on them again.

We relocated and set up our home in sunny AZ and things began to look up. I started making more money than I had ever made legally in my life. We got an apartment and Jay got an amazing job with Coca-Cola. Things couldn't be better, but somehow in my mind that still wasn't enough and I felt like I was failing. I mean I was finally able to walk with my chin up but part of me was just going through the motions because I missed my twins so much. They should have been able to reap the benefits of my change too. The day I had waited for happened, my son had reached out and said he wanted to come home. I immediately purchased a ticket and got him to AZ. Sadly my daughter was not ready to leave her friends or school, so I had to just deal with having one back in my life. I set my son up for school, and things were finally feeling like they should have. As things in AZ started to become our new norm, I started back focusing on my healing. Sometimes it's not enough to just do the work. I found that sharing my story was therapeutic for me. I started using my profile on social media for healing. I started to share pieces of my story and was surprised at the amount of people that had a very similar story to mine. I was finally feeling like I was walking in my healing. I was doing well but I couldn't help but think of ways to get revenge on my ex-husband. I wanted him to hurt the way he had hurt me. Little did I know he was hurting for other reasons. Life had not been kind to him at all and I soon came to find out just how bad things were. I remember it just like it was yesterday. I was in my room folding clothes when a call came from a 202 number. I knew that area code because I had called so many attorneys in that area when the kids first got taken. I honestly was not prepared for what would come after I picked up the phone. The caller on the other line said, "Hey, you don't know me, but I think we need to talk." She introduced herself and stated that her and D were dating, and they fell out a while back. She continued to say that she knew for a fact that my daughter and her father were living in his van for a long while. My stomach dropped. I simply could not believe that he would take my children to get back at me even though he knew he could not afford to take care of them. She said that she couldn't continue to let her live in the car so she made them come stay at her house because he wouldn't allow her to stay if he couldn't come. They stayed but she was tired of him and made him leave and that's where her drama started with him. I don't know if she called me as a get back to him, but honestly, I didn't really care. She told me that she started putting the stories together and realized he had been lying for years about what really happened and how he got the kids. I didn't know whether to be angry or relieved my nightmare was finally ending. I was both. I was relieved that he was struggling and happy to know that he was not happy, but I was equally sad that my daughter had to go through an unnecessary struggle. I sent for my daughter immediately! She didn't want to leave for two weeks so she could have a chance to say bye to everyone and the lady that called me offered my daughter the ability to stay at her house while she was getting things ready to come to AZ. Life had finally started to look up for me. Things had finally started to fall in place.

My mom saw the change in me and even till this day she reminds me of how proud she is of me. I was finally where I wanted to be, but it still wasn't good enough for me. I needed D to see that I was doing well despite his attempts to make sure I failed. I wanted him to acknowledge that he did in fact drag me through the mud and tortured me because he was bitter. I needed him to suffer the way I did. My moment came, but before that I got a preview of what humble pie looks like and I was so pleased. While I was waiting on the two weeks to pass, I got a text from D and I almost thought he had the wrong number. This nigga had the audacity to ask to borrow $500 from me. I was floored and humored. I mean, I said I was healing not healed. I was so excited to tell his bitch ass…. FUCK NO! He said he needed it to get his tags or something so he could drive legally. I knew he'd be driving around with my daughter in the vehicle, and I didn't want her to watch her father go to jail for driving dirty. I also didn't know if she would be able to get to a safe space if he did get pulled over. The bitch in me wanted to say no, but the petty in me said "Let me ask my HUSBAND if its ok." I sent the money and gave him a deadline. I sent him a reminder daily that he owed me. I mean imagine you dragging me for years just to have to need me. GOD do not play about me; he be sick of me but he don't play! I didn't even have to get him back, the universe aligned and did it for me. I had every reason to say no. I even recall the time it was my year to file the kids for taxes and I submitted and got rejected because he went behind my back and filed them. I mean he gave me no reasons that would make me want to loan him the money, but I did.

D ended up sending me a text a few days later saying he would have my money for me next Friday and that he also wanted to talk to me when he did. I agreed because I had every intention on unloading on him. Friday came and he called. I put him on speaker because I just needed my husband to know that everything, I told him about D was true, even though I knew he believed me. I needed someone to know that he did this because he was bitter not because he felt like the kids were in danger. I waited 3 years for this moment. D began to apologize for everything. He said that he was upset about me packing up and leaving him in 2005. He also stated that the determining factor was him coming to my house and seeing that I was pregnant by someone else. He said he started thinking of ways to make me hurt. He said that he was dealing with some things and life wasn't going well for him. He had kidnapped our kids because he was bitter over a marriage that ended 11 years prior. He even said there were so many times he wanted to call me and tell me he was thinking of me or wanted to tell me a joke that he thought was funny….as if I would ever take his calls. I had waited years for this moment and all I could feel was heat. I didn't feel relieved like I thought I would. I could only think of how I wished I would have recorded it so I could let my mom and aunt listen to it. I wanted the world to know that the picture he painted of me was wrong, but I would have to settle for just having Jay hear it. D was a coward and somehow, I had to be ok with the apology his wack ass had just given. I just expected to feel different.

Despite the wack apology I got, life started moving forward and things continuously began to fall in place for me and my family. Things have been going great and I'd like to think that I have healed fully but that couldn't be further from the truth. I got my kids back, I was no longer dealing with my father, my demons had been silenced, and I was confronting my own toxicity so things should have been so much better now, right? NOT!! See the thing about healing is that it's not a one and done. Most times you don't get to just cleanse and move on. Self-talk is real and baby if I told you about all the negative conversations, I had with myself about myself, this book would be bible long. I mentioned a while back that I was the queen of faking it until I made it and I am, but once you acknowledge your bad traits, they become that much harder to hide.

My kids being back was a big win for me. Now that I had them back, I wanted everyone to go back and admit they had no business siding with D. They had no business making me feel like I had done something wrong. I was looking for acknowledgement of what I had been saying from day 1, but I wasn't getting it. It was always in favor of him no matter what. You have no idea how many times I heard "Well one thing about D is he loves them twins" or "Maybe he just kind of lost control of the situation." The blood inside of me boils over every time I think about it. I am a right fighter and I know that them not acknowledging the fact that D was a horrible person hindered me from growing and truly healing. I soon began to understand that I was definitely looking for acknowledgement, but I was also looking for closure. The same way D opened pandoras box and spewed my business to anybody that would listen, was the same way I needed it to close. I had started following my father on social media and it was definitely a trigger for me. My husband always asks why I don't just delete him from my social media, so I don't have to see the exact thing I have no desire to see. I really didn't have any answer honestly. My father and I had built a generic relationship a few years back, but it was never genuine honestly. It always felt forced but for some reason I think that I stay connected because I know that once I delete him, he won't ever reach out to me and that makes it final and very real. For me, as much as I despise him that's a hard pill to swallow.

It was easy for me to recognize that some of my hurt was self-inflicted but very hard to accept it. Have you ever seen a victim in a scary movie chasing the monster? I never have! Looking back on my life I felt like I have been tracking and chasing down my monsters trying to catch them so they could say sorry to me for trying to kill me. Once I reached that monster, I would be so appalled that they would take out their hatchet and try and kill me again. I was literally looking for compassion and love from the boogie man. This behavior is really a form of insanity. I learned later in the healing game that closure was not even a reality for me, especially if I was considering getting it from the people that caused chaos and turmoil in my life. I had made the conscious decision to start incorporating activities that allowed me to not only express but also begin my healing process. I started with journaling and being as real and raw as possible. Sometimes I felt like I was just stating the obvious, and for me it worked a bit, but I felt like I needed more. The people I needed closure from would not be giving it to me, so I took matters into my own hands. I began writing letters to the people that hurt me the most and the relief I felt was amazing. I knew that I would never get a response, nor would they ever be able to read it but being able to get my thoughts out as if I were talking to them provided me the closure I needed. Some letters I had to apologize to old friends, and other letters I was saying things I was too scared to say out loud. I had finally got the release and the closure I needed. I began to pick out the things I still hated about myself and combat them with positive affirmations each morning. OMG I was finally moving in the right direction, and I didn't have to wait on anyone to help me get there. One of the things I had always struggled with was betting on self and I was conquering that one day at a time. That box that I had kept myself in for so many years no longer made me feel safe it suddenly made me feel small and silenced and it no longer served any purpose useful to me.

FORGET YOUR FAILURES, FORGIVE YOURSELF!

Forgiving myself was probably one of the hardest parts of my journey but it was one that I knew I deserved. One of the hardest obstacles after healing was me beating myself up over the mistakes I made, and I had made too many to keep track of. I finally grasped that I can't go back in time and re-write history but what I could do was be better moving forward and that is just what I did. For the longest time I would allow people to try and hold me emotionally and mentally hostage where they remembered me in my past, even though they could clearly see the change in me. I knew now more than ever that I had to use my voice to correct them if I ever wanted to be able to move forward in a healthy way. The more I did it, the more comfortable I got with checking them. I quickly learned that sometimes a sincere apology and self-correction is not enough for the person that you hurt, but I realized I was not required to shrink myself for their satisfaction and comfortability. My favorite lesson was that "NO" was a complete sentence that required no explanation, and I no longer had to say yes out of guilt. I had always heard that to grow you must shed some weight, but I never imagined it would be the weight of people you once considered friends or family. It was a harsh reality, but I was ok with it. The people who couldn't accept that I had changed for the better slowly removed themselves from my life and I didn't have to lift a finger. I had worked so hard on changing myself that I didn't have any more time or energy to help change the way someone thought of me, especially when I was a walking billboard of change. As long as I knew I had corrected my errors and sincerely apologized, I was ok with shedding the dead weight of fake relationships. I worked hard to become an upstanding woman and I refused to let myself or anyone else keep me in the box of my old life. For once in my life, I no longer allowed my past decisions to define my future life. I was now comfortable in my own skin, living the way I wanted to, unapologetically, and you couldn't pay me any amount of money to change that. I had started to choose me! My journey isn't anywhere close to being complete and I still have a lot to learn, but I am ready to take on the world, eyes wide open. I forgive me, and I hope those that I have wronged or hurt will too. The future is looking really good, and I am in a place to receive all things meant for me. My biggest take away from my life is that hurt people hurt people, broken people break people, and healed people heal people...Which one describes you?

www.ingramcontent.com/pod-product-compliance
Lightning Source LLC
Chambersburg PA
CBHW072008290426
44109CB00018B/2175